CELEBRATING

JTBD **25** ODI

1991 - 2016

ISBN# 978-0-9905767-4-7

Published by IDEA BITE PRESS
www.ideabitepress.com
Printed in the United States of America

"**Anthony Ulwick** has taken the guesswork out of innovation. For 25 years he has worked to guide companies to success. He has done this by introducing us to **Jobs-to-be-Done theory**, and converting it to practice using his rigorous innovation process known as **Outcome-Driven Innovation**.

The vast majority of innovation projects fail. With Ulwick's process we finally learn what the best know already - ***innovation cannot be left to chance.*** It can and should be managed for successful outcomes.

I call him the **Deming of Innovation** because, more than anyone else, Tony has turned innovation into a science."

Philip Kotler

S. C. Johnson Distinguished Professor of International Marketing at the Kellogg School of Management, Northwestern University

"We are committed devotees. Our innovation teams have seen the Outcome-Driven Innovation process work not just once, but over and over again. Without a doubt, it brings predictability to innovation and contributes to growth."

Clive Meanwell

Chief Executive Officer, Chairman, The Medicines Company

"In *What Customers Want*, Tony Ulwick redefined how innovators think about their customers. His importance and satisfaction framework for a customer's "jobs to be done" has influenced a generation of marketing and innovation professionals. Now with *Jobs to be Done: Theory to Practice*, we get the refined version, based on a decade of Tony's learnings applying the framework."

Michael Wynblatt

Ph.D., Vice President of Innovation, Ingersoll Rand

"Outcome-Driven Innovation's customer-centric approach to innovation and product design helps us define and address truly important client challenges. That additional clarity further enables us to develop and deliver solutions that provide real customer value, as well as deep, ongoing benefits to my organization and me. Our understanding of client needs and how to gain insight into those needs has been greatly improved."

Alex Johnson
System Architect - Next Generation Systems of Process Automation, Schneider Electric

"I've had the privilege to work with Tony and his team across two different organizations. Each time he has elevated our thinking and brought us a way to drive innovation that is radically different from traditional methods. It has been a great journey watching our team think and act with a focus on customer-centric outcomes."

Frank Grillo
Chief Marketing Officer, Harte Hanks

"Jobs Theory and Outcome-Driven Innovation have proven to be highly valuable in the development of innovative pharmaceuticals. A focus on the 'job' brings clarity to the complex healthcare delivery process and reveals hidden opportunities to positively impact the patients' pathway to health."

Simona Skerjanec
Lifecycle Leader – Neuroscience, Roche

"Outcome-Driven Innovation unlocks unique insights into your customers and their challenges. It impacts revenue growth through new product development and identification of new customer segments."

Joe Camaratta
Managing Director, MedTech Playbook

"Jobs-to-be-Done Theory and Outcome-Driven Innovation provide absolute clarity for strategic growth initiatives and product innovation. There is no better way to put yourself in your customers' shoes."

Steve Thompson

Vice President of Business Strategy, National Oilwell Varco

"Acquiring technologies for developing new medical products has always been an exercise in trying to guess correctly. ODI has provided us with an enabling technology shopping list we can execute with confidence. ODI makes Business Development far more precise."

Sean Thompson, MS, MBA, CLP

Sr. Director, Business Operations & New Product Development, GenCure

"The Jobs-To-Be-Done approach drove within us a heightened focus on our customers. We discovered important and often "unspoken" customer needs. Even in established markets, we gained new insights enabling stronger value propositions, more impactful customer communications, and innovation better aligned with market needs."

David Rusinko

Director Strategic Marketing, Momentive

"The ODI process provides broad and detailed customer insights that are superior to typical market research methods and critical to developing better solutions for customers. ODI helped us understand a new space and identify the underserved needs so we could enter a new market in a differentiated manner."

Brian Craig

VP of Strategy and Business Development, Surgical Innovations, Medtronic

CONTENTS

All companies want to satisfy their customer's needs. So what is standing in the way? The problem is there is no agreement on what a "need" even is.

A key implication of Jobs-to-be-Done Theory is that it provides a framework for categorizing, defining, capturing and organizing the 6 types of customer needs.

- The Core Functional Job-to-be-Done
- Desired Outcomes On the Core Functional Job
- Related Jobs
- Emotional and Social Jobs
- Consumption Chain Jobs
- Financial Desired Outcomes

New products and services win when they get a job done better and/or more cheaply. This observation leads to five unique growth strategies companies can employ to address opportunities in a market.

- Differentiated Strategy
- Dominant Strategy

- Disruptive Strategy
- Discrete Strategy
- Sustaining Strategy

PROCESS

4. OUTCOME-DRIVEN INNOVATION®

Following the Outcome-Driven Innovation® (ODI) process enables companies to conceptualize new solutions that help customers get a job done better and/or more cheaply. It has an 86% success rate because it begins with a deep understanding of the Job-to-be-Done and employs unique quantitative research methods that enable companies to analyze markets in ways that have never before been possible.

    I.   Define the Customer
    II.   Define the Job-to-be-Done
    III.   Uncover Customer Needs
          - The Universal Job Map
          - The Desired Outcome Statement
    IV.   Find Segments of Opportunity
    V.   Define the Value Proposition
    VI.   Conduct the Competitive Analysis
    VII.   Formulate the Innovation Strategy
    VIII.   Target Hidden Growth Opportunities
          - The Opportunity Algorithm
          - The Opportunity Landscape
    IX.   Formulate the Market Strategy
    X.   Formulate the Product Strategy

5. CASE STUDIES

The ODI process has been employed throughout the world in hundreds of companies. Here are a few stories that describe the ODI process in action, what hidden opportunities the process reveals, and the results it delivers.

- Microsoft
- Kroll Ontrack
- Arm & Hammer
- Bosch
- Abbott Medical Optics
- Hussmann

PRACTICE

6. BECOMING AN ODI PRACTITIONER

To effectively execute an ODI project, an ODI practitioner must have the skills and instruction to do so. Listed in this chapter are the 84 steps an ODI practitioner must execute to produce a winning outcome-driven growth strategy. Learn what it takes to put Jobs-to-be-Done Theory into practice and become an effective ODI practitioner.

7. TRANSFORMING THE ORGANIZATION

Putting Jobs-to-be-Done Theory and ODI into practice is not easy, but let's not make it harder than it needs to be. Using a three-phased approach, a company is able to see its markets through a new lens, obtain customer insights that have previously been impossible to obtain, and use them to drive growth through innovation.

I. Understand Your Customer's Job-to-be-Done

II. Discover Hidden Opportunities In Your Market

III. Use New Customer Insights to Drive Growth

A recent research study by pricing firm Simon-Kucher & Partners shows that **72% of all new product & service introductions fail to live up to expectations.** It doesn't have to be that way. The right tools, processes, and organizational structures can help companies better navigate today's challenging, ever changing, and dynamic business environment. This book contributes an important piece to the equation of how companies can avoid falling victim to disruption by smaller or newer players in the market.

When I started working on business model innovation, I quickly realized that business practitioners needed simple, practical, and intuitive tools to do a better job at coming up with new business models. We needed a shared language. And that's why we designed tools like the **Business Model Canvas**, **Value Proposition Canvas**, and **Culture Map** to provide a shared language for communicating complex topics and making them tangible.

The importance of process and tools cannot be overstated. Process drives efficiency. Tools create a guided framework for conversations. They encourage participants to collaborate in different environments, and perhaps most importantly, they encourage participants to discuss something tangible. However, the tools, processes, and culture required for successful innovation differ from those applied today to guarantee the successful execution and improvement of known business models and value propositions.

Companies that don't want their future prosperity to suffer at the expense of present success need to complement their execution-focused toolbox and mindset with an innovation-focused toolbox and mindset. **Tony Ulwick** and his team at **Strategyn** provide an important part of this toolbox.

I learned to appreciate Tony Ulwick's work when I dove deeper into the Jobs-to-be-Done concept via Professor Clayton Christensen book, *The Innovator's Solution* (Harvard Business School Press, 2003), and Tony's article *The Customer-Centered Innovation Map* (Harvard Business Review, 2008). Subsequently, I discovered Strategyn's powerful Outcome-Driven Innovation (ODI) process that companies can use to effectively execute the innovation process. ***Ultimately, this research led my team and me to design the Value Proposition Canvas.***

I've studied Tony's work over the years and come to appreciate how the process is able to effectively take a lot of the guesswork out of the innovation process. Tony has succeeded in bringing us a **tested model and framework for innovation management** that greatly increases the probability of success. It is an important part of the equation of how companies can avoid getting disrupted and successfully fight off competitors by obsessing over what really matters to customers.

Read this book to substantially improve your innovation toolbox and process. It shows you what to do (and what to avoid) in order to succeed.

Alex Osterwalder
Founder, Strategyzer
October, 2016

INTRODUCTION:
THE FAILURE THAT LED TO SUCCESS

INSPIRED BY FAILURE

Early in my career as a product engineer, I experienced the ultimate professional disappointment: for 18 months I put my heart and soul into creating a product that failed in the marketplace.

It was 1984, and I was part of the IBM PCjr development team. We were working on a product that was supposed to revolutionize home computing. In advance of its release, the *Washington Post* wrote, "the PCjr will quickly become the standard by which all other home computers are measured." So you can imagine my surprise when, the day after we introduced the PCjr, I woke up to read the headlines in the *Wall Street Journal* declaring, **"PCjr is a flop."**

I was shocked! As we learned over the next few months, they were right. It was a flop, an embarrassment that cost IBM over a billion dollars and put a blemish on its reputation.

The **humiliation of failure** had a profound effect on me. I was determined to never let that happen again. In the weeks that followed I wondered how the *Wall Street Journal* had been able to see this correctly, and so quickly. It occurred to me that if we knew what metrics they (and potential customers) were going to use to judge the value of our product well before we introduced it, we would have the opportunity to design our product to address those metrics and achieve a positive result.

This set me on a mission: *I wanted to figure out a way to **identify the metrics** that customers use to **judge the value** of newly released products early on in the product planning process.*

THE BREAKTHROUGH

Over the next five years, I studied and tried out many new tools that looked promising, including voice of the customer, quality function deployment (QFD), TRIZ, Six Sigma, and conjoint analysis. I studied everything that was written about these tools and used them in my product planning activities. I conducted hundreds of customer interviews and dozens of quantitative studies. I also worked with IBM statisticians to learn how to best apply conjoint, factor, and cluster analysis to segment markets in a meaningful way. I worked as an internal IBM consultant, using what I learned to help different internal teams formulate market and product strategies. IBM management was very supportive throughout this process, which is something I appreciate to this day.

It was in North Sydney, Australia, with an IBM team in 1990 when I had a mental breakthrough. Six Sigma thinking seeks to improve the quality of the output of a process by identifying and removing the causes of defects. It uses a set of quality management methods, mainly empirical, statistical methods, to address process deficiencies. It occurred to me that we could apply *Six Sigma and process control principles to innovation* if we studied the process that people were trying to execute when they were using a product or service, rather than studying the product itself. Once we made the process the subject of our investigation, we'd be able to break it down into process steps, study each step in detail, and attach metrics to each step that we could measure and control in the design of a product.

I was so excited about this prospect that I struggled to sleep for days. As I thought about it more, I realized that to make this work I would have to figure out **how to uncover the metrics that customers use to measure success** and value as they go about executing these processes.

VALIDATING THE PROCESS

In October 1991, I left IBM and founded The Total Quality Group. The goal of this one-man consultancy was to apply my newly envisioned process, which I called CD-MAP (to denote the concept of *customer-driven maps*), to product strategy and planning initiatives.

One of my first clients was **Cordis Corporation**, a company that was trying to reinvent its line of angioplasty balloon products. I interviewed interventional cardiologists to break down and analyze the process they went through to "restore blood flow in a blocked artery." Through this qualitative research effort, I carefully constructed 75 uniquely defined customer need statements that I called desired outcomes. The statements described the metrics that interventional cardiologists were using to judge and measure their success as they tried to restore blood flow in an artery. With these customer-defined metrics in hand, I conducted quantitative research to discover which of those outcomes were underserved—important to the interventional cardiologists, but not well satisfied. I discovered several.

I then facilitated a series of strategy sessions to help the Cordis team use these insights to create a new product line. By mid-1993, the company launched 19 new products, all of which became number 1 or 2 in the market.

Cordis' market share increased from 1 percent to more than 20 percent, and its stock price more than quadrupled. Needless to say, I was thrilled: this was validation that my method worked. Tying customer-defined metrics to the underlying process the customer was trying to execute was the key to success.

ADVANCING THE PROCESS

I engaged in dozens of innovation initiatives over the next several years, achieving similar results with companies such as Motorola, Pratt & Whitney, Medtronic, AIG, Allied Signal and Telectronics. Making process refinements with every application, I learned how to apply the process in multiple industries and for hardware, software, and service offerings. The process became very robust as I continued to rid it of inefficiencies and variability and established a strict set of rules for defining desired outcome statements. As the decade progressed, I decided to rename the company and offering to communicate its focus on strategy and innovation, and in 1999, the company became **Strategyn** and the data-driven process became **Outcome-Driven Innovation®** **(ODI)**.

Also in 1999 I was granted my first patent on the ODI process. It was the first of 12 patents I would eventually receive regarding my strategy and innovation process.

In late 1999, I had the distinct pleasure of introducing **Outcome-Driven Innovation** and our research and segmentation techniques to Harvard Business School professor **Clayton Christensen.** We met in his Harvard office on several occasions in the 5 years that followed. I introduced Clay to ODI and showed him examples of how the process was executed and the results it delivered our clients.

Clay was quick to key in on the fact that the focus of our approach was not on the customer or the product, but rather on the underlying process the customer was trying to execute, or, as he eventually came to call it, *the "job" the customer was trying to get done.*

Clay was kind enough to cite Strategyn and me as originators of these practices in his 2003 book, *The Innovator's Solution*, in which he popularized the idea that people "hire" products to get a "job" done. To this day, Clay continues to be a proponent of Jobs-to-be-Done Theory and a key contributor to its development.

Clay also introduced me to Mark Johnson and Matt Eyring, who I enjoyed working with on a number of joint activities in the early days of Innosight. I was honored that an offer was made to me to join Innosight as a partner in 2004, although I respectfully declined the offer. While Innosight's focus on disruptive innovation was exciting, my focus on Jobs-to-be-Done theory and ODI remained my top priority.

In 2002, *Harvard Business Review* (HBR) published my article called ***Turn Customer Input into Innovation***, which described Outcome-Driven Innovation and its successful application at Cordis. The success of that article helped our team to grow Strategyn as a business and inspired me to write a book on Outcome-Driven Innovation called ***What Customers Want: Using Outcome-Driven Innovation to Create Breakthrough Products***. Released in 2005, this seminal book explained in detail how ODI transforms Jobs-to-be-Done Theory into an effective innovation practice. Since that time I have had the honor of writing other articles that were published in *HBR* and *MIT Sloan Management Review*.

The most rewarding part of my journey has resulted from being a hands-on ODI **practitioner**. That is my passion. I have led and continue to lead hundreds of innovation engagements with inspiring people in the world's most admired companies. Every week I have the privilege of learning from top thinkers in companies across a wide range of industries. In 2016, the Strategyn team and I have worked with companies such as B. Braun, HD Supply, Minitab, Twitter, Panasonic, Kawasaki, WL Gore, Momentive, The Medicines Company, Roche, Bayer, P&G, Medtronic, Oracle, Johnson & Johnson, Arm & Hammer, Harte Hanks, DePuy, Terumo, CA Technologies, and Pulte Group. I am a practitioner at heart.

Years of hands-on experience applying ODI have been the key to continued process improvement and our advancement of Jobs-to-be-Done Theory. To this day my team and I have ongoing ODI best practice reviews to share our collective knowledge and improve our thinking, tools and practices. **Our goal remains the same—to transform innovation from an art to a science.**

In the September, 2016 *Harvard Business Review* article, *Know Your Customers' Jobs to be Done*, **Clayton Christensen** states, "Innovation can be far more predictable—and far more profitable—if you start by identifying the jobs that customers are struggling to get done".

Strategyn has collected data through formal research that supports Christensen's claim and shows just how much more predictable innovation becomes when using Jobs-to-be-Done Theory and Outcome-Driven Innovation.

To obtain this data, we engaged a Harvard Business School trained independent researcher to study the success rates of traditional innovation methods vs. our own innovation process, **Outcome-Driven Innovation.**

The results of that study showed that while the success rates of traditional innovation processes average **17 percent**, the success rate of **Outcome-Driven Innovation** is **86 percent**.

This means that 86 percent of the products and services launched by our clients using ODI were a success. This data validates Christensen's claim that the innovation process is more predictable if you start with a focus on the Job-to-be-Done. In fact, **it is five-times more predictable**. The reason for the success of ODI is simple: a company can dramatically increase its chances for success at innovation if it knows precisely what metrics customers use to measure success and value when getting a job done.

Here are the details of the study.

JOBS-TO-BE-DONE THEORY & OUTCOME-DRIVEN INNOVATION IMPROVES INNOVATION SUCCESS RATES

In order to accurately determine the success rate for traditional innovation processes, the researcher found success rate reports from 12 different sources, including the *Harvard Business Review*, the consulting firm Frost & Sullivan, the professional services firm PricewaterhouseCoopers, the Product Development Management Association (PDMA), the Corporate Strategy Board and others.

- **Frost & Sullivan** reported (i) that *only one in 300 new products* significantly impacts a company's growth and (ii) that **only 1% of new products recoup** their **product development costs**.

- The **Corporate Strategy Board** reported that over the past four decades, of the 172 companies that spent time in the Fortune 50, **only 5% sustained a growth rate greater than the growth rate of the gross domestic product**.

- PricewaterhouseCoopers reported that only **11% of all venture investments get to any capital liquidity**.

- **R.G. Cooper** reported that new products succeed **25%** of the time.

- The **Product Development Management Association (PDMA)** claims that new products succeed **59%** of the time.

The 12 sources studied and the innovation success rates they cited are summarized in the table:

Source	Rate
Frost & Sullivan, "Growth Process Toolkit: New Product Development," 2008.	0.3%
Frost & Sullivan, "Growth Process Toolkit: New Product Development," 2008.	1%
Andrew Campbell and Robert Park, 'Stop Kissing Frogs," *Harvard Business Review*, July-August 2004.	1%
Dr. John Sviokla, "The Calculus of Commerce," Diamond Cluster International, Inc. 2004.	3%
Corporate Strategy Board, "Stall Points," 1998. Cited in Clayton Christensen and Michael Raynor, "The Innovator's Solution," page 5, *Harvard Business School Press,* 2003.	5%
Andrew Campbell and Robert Park, 'Stop Kissing Frogs," *Harvard Business Review*, July-August 2004.	10%
Kevin J. Clancy and Randy L. Stone, "Don't Blame the Metrics," *Harvard Business Review*, June 2005.	10%
Corporate Strategy Board, "Overcoming Stall Pints," 2006.	10%
PriceWaterHouseCoopers, "Shaking the Money-Tree," slide 33, U.S. Venture Liquidity 2001-2007, Q3 2008.	11%
Average	17%
Dr. Robert G. Cooper, "Doing it Right," Product Development Institute Inc., 2006.	25%
Abbie Griffin, "Drivers of New Products Success," Product Development & Management Association, 1997.	59%
Dr. Robert G. Cooper, "Doing it Right," Product Development Institute Inc., 2006.	67%
Strategyn	**86%**

In order to study the success rate of our Outcome-Driven Innovation methodology, the researcher conducted interviews with representatives of 43 Strategyn clients that had used ODI to launch a product or service or to engage in an operational or marketing innovation initiative. No incentives were offered to those who participated, and to encourage candor, anonymity was assured.

The researcher asked companies to judge the success of the ODI initiative they undertook based on their choice of one of four success metrics: **revenue**, **market share**, **customer satisfaction**, or **return on investment**. The company representative was re-contacted to confirm agreement with the categorizations (i.e., successful or unsuccessful, the success metrics used, etc.).

Of 21 projects that made use of the ODI methodology and resulted in product launches, 18 were rated successes by the sponsoring company—an **86% success rate**. *Five of these product launches received industry awards.* I'll describe some of these projects as case studies for success later in this book.

Strategyn clients interviewed	43
ODI-based products entered into development	49
Pending launch	28
Launched	21
Declared a success after launch	18
Success Rate	**86%**

The 21 launches were categorized as follows: new product (10), new service (1), product enhancement (4), service enhancement (4), and operational enhancement (2). For the three product launches that were considered unsuccessful, the sponsoring companies indicated that they did a poor job of executing the commercialization of the product.

Company	Industry	What was launched	Success Criteria	Case Study	Award	Success
Company A	Medical devices	New product	Revenue	✔		✔
Company B	Hardware	New product	Market share	✔	✔	✔
Company C	Software	New product	Revenue			
Company D	Financial services	New product	Customer Sat			✔
Company E	Industrial	New product	Revenue			✔
Company F	Medical devices	New product	Revenue	✔		✔
Company F	Medical devices	New product	Customer Sat	✔	✔	✔
Company G	Software	New product	Revenue	✔	✔	✔
Company H	Consumer electronics	New product	Revenue	✔		
Company I	Hardware	New product	Market share		✔	✔
Company J	Manufacturing	New service	Customer Sat			✔
Company F	Medical devices	Product enhancement	Revenue			✔
Company F	Medical devices	Product enhancement	Revenue			
Company K	Software	Product enhancement	Revenue	✔		✔
Company K	Software	Product enhancement	Revenue			✔
Company L	Medical devices	Service enhancement	Customer Satisfaction	✔	✔	✔
Company M	Business services	Service enhancement	Customer Satisfaction			✔
Company N	Financial services	Service enhancement	Customer Satisfaction			✔
Company O	Emergency services	Service enhancement	Revenue			✔
Company P	Aviation	Operational enhancement	ROI			✔
Company P	Aviation	Operational enhancement	ROI			✔
Subtotals				8	5	18
Total						21
Success Rate						86%

THIS BOOK

"What is the value of Jobs-to-be-Done Theory and how do you put the theory into practice?"

This book answers these questions. I reveal to you the hidden implications of Jobs-to-be-Done Theory and explain how to put Jobs-to-be-Done Theory into practice using **Outcome-Driven Innovation®.**

The structure of this book systematically takes you through three phases – from **Theory**, to **Process** and finally to **Practice**.

The story told in this book can be summarized as follows:

- Companies fail frequently at innovation because they struggle to understand and rationalize all the customer's needs.

- Jobs Theory provides a needs framework that makes it possible to categorize, define, capture, organize and prioritize customer needs.

- A strategy framework, built around Jobs Theory, enables a company to correctly categorize, understand, and employ the 5 strategies that drive growth.

- Outcome-Driven Innovation ties customer-defined metrics to the customer's Job-to-be-Done, transforming every aspect of opportunity discovery, marketing and innovation.
- Prospective practitioners can assess their ability to put Jobs Theory and ODI into practice with detailed insight into a typical innovation initiative.
- Companies should employ a proven three-phased approach to build a competency in Outcome-Driven Innovation.

Chapter 1 introduces us to the root cause of failure in innovation. Why do so many projects fail?

Chapter 2 introduces the solution: the Job-to-be-Done Needs Framework.

Chapter 3 introduces the Job-to-be-Done Growth Strategy Matrix to explain how and when to use the five strategies that drive growth.

Chapter 4 introduces our latest thinking regarding the execution of the Outcome-Driven Innovation process.

Chapter 5 includes six case studies of companies that applied the Outcome-Driven Innovation process and achieved impressive results.

Starting with **Chapter 6**, we introduce the Practice: **a description of the 84 steps that comprise the Outcome-Driven Innovation process.** Developed over the past 25 years, these are the steps a practitioner must take to successfully execute ODI.

Chapter 7 describes a three-phased approach for helping your organization use ODI to build a competency in innovation.

Chapter 8 is about the "Language of Job-to-be-Done" – the lexicon of innovation.

Lastly, **Chapter 9** points you to useful resources – videos, articles, and books that may be helpful on your journey of learning and practice.

Innovation is far from simple.

An **effective innovation process** must produce answers to the following questions:

1. Who is the customer?
2. What job is the customer trying to get done?
3. What are the customer's desired outcomes?
4. How do they measure value?
5. Do segments of customers exist that have different unmet outcomes?
6. What unmet outcomes exist in each segment?

7. What segments and unmet outcomes should we target for growth?
8. How should we define our value proposition?
9. How should we position our existing and pipeline products?
10. What new products must we create?

The qualitative, quantitative, and analytical methods that comprise our **Outcome-Driven Innovation®** process reveal answers to these questions and more.

ODI replaces luck with a predictable process.

This book is part of my lifelong journey. For the **past 25 years**, I've worked with the best and brightest people in industry, and have seen innovation through the lens of many companies. I've had the privilege of contributing to the creation of products that save and protect lives and other products that make those lives more enjoyable.

It is my sincere hope that this book will help you and your organization on your quest for innovation success. Contact me to share your stories and insights: *ulwick@strategyn.com*.

THEORY

1.
WHY DO INNOVATION PROJECTS FAIL?

The goal of innovation is straightforward: to come up with solutions that address unmet customer needs. Today's most popular approaches to innovation fall into one of two types: those that begin with a focus on solutions (or ideas) and those that begin with a focus on customer needs.

In what I call the "ideas-first" approach, companies brainstorm or otherwise come up with product or service ideas and then test them with customers to see how well the ideas address the customer's needs. In the "needs-first" approach, companies first learn what the customer's needs are, then discover which needs are unmet, and then devise a solution that addresses those unmet needs.

As I will explain, the "ideas-first" approach is inherently flawed and will never be the most effective approach to innovation. It will always be a guessing game that is based on hope and luck, and it will remain unpredictable. The "needs-first" approach to innovation, while not inherently flawed, is often flawed in its execution. Recognizing why it is flawed and executing it correctly is the key to success in innovation. This structural flaw in the needs-first approach is corrected in the **Outcome-Driven Innovation** process.

THE IDEAS-FIRST APPROACH IS INHERENTLY FLAWED

Many companies adhere to the "ideas-first" approach and have developed support systems and organizational cultures that reinforce its use. Companies that follow this paradigm believe that the key to success in innovation is to be able to generate a large number of ideas (the more, the better) and to be able to quickly and inexpensively filter out the ideas that will likely fail. They believe this approach gives them a better chance of coming up with a greater number of breakthrough ideas.

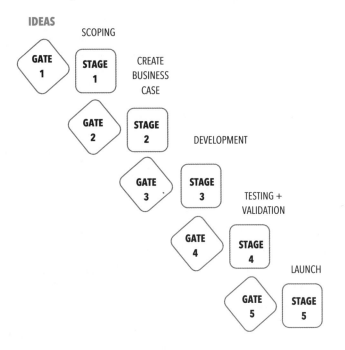

Many academics, managers, and consultants support this thinking. Creators and supporters of many of the popular gated or "phase gate" development processes, for example, state that the first step of the development process is idea generation.

Approximately 68 percent of large businesses have adopted some form of gated development, which means that this same percentage have adopted, at least to some degree, the ideas-first mentality. *[Robert Cooper, "Winning at New Products: Accelerating the Process from Idea to Launch," 3rd ed. (Da Capo Press, 2001), 311.]* Examples demonstrating the prevalence of this mind-set abound.

In their book, *Innovation to the Core*, Strategos CEO **Peter Skarzynski** and Rowan Gibson say that **"successful innovation is a numbers game... the chance of finding a big, new opportunity is very much a function of how many ideas you generate, how many you pick out and test with low-cost experiments."** *[Peter Skarzynski and Rowan Gibson, "Innovation to the Core" (Chicago: Strategos, 2008), 137.]*

Harvard Business School professor **Teresa Amabile** states in a frequently cited article that **"all innovation begins with creative ideas."** *[Teresa M. Amabile, Regina Conti, Heather Coon, Jeffrey Lazenby, and Michael Herron, "Assessing the Work Environment for Creativity," Academy of Management Journal 39, no. 5 (October 1996), 1154.]*

Nearly everyone in a major corporation has participated in a brainstorming session in which, without knowing the customer's needs, they were encouraged to generate hundreds of ideas and were told that there is no such thing as a bad idea. You can probably still picture walls of Post-It notes.

Others who support the ideas-first approach have promoted the benefits of executing the approach quickly. Many refer to this accelerated ideas-first approach as "failing fast," the idea being that when many ideas are generated and tested quickly, the best ideas are revealed faster. Since it is accepted that an ideas-first approach is going to generate many failures, it seems logical to try and weed out the failures quickly.

This concept was touted by **Tom Peters** in *Thriving on Chaos*. Peters said companies should, **"test fast, fail fast, adjust fast—pursue new business ideas on a small scale and in a way that generates quick feedback about whether an idea is viable."** *[Tom Peters, Thriving on Chaos: Handbook for a Management Revolution (New York: Knopf/Random House, 1987), 479.]*

IBM founder Thomas Watson, who years ago said, **"If you want to succeed, double your failure rate,"** also supported this thinking and adopted a management style that did not punish failure.

The fail-fast approach is still well supported today. For example, the authors of the recently published *Innovators Guide to Growth* believe that **"if you fail fast and fail cheap, you have actually done your company a great service."** *[Scott D. Anthony, Mark W. Johnson, Joseph V. Sinfield, and Elizabeth J. Altman, The Innovator's Guide to Growth, Putting Disruptive Innovation to Work, (Harvard Business Press, 2008), 94.]*

As a result of this ideas-first thinking, an entire ideation industry has evolved to compete on developing ways to generate and evaluate more and more ideas, faster and faster.

But there is a problem: despite its popularity, academic support, and widespread use, the ideas-first approach to innovation cannot be counted on for predictable growth and is inherently doomed to failure.

There are three reasons for this:

First, **generating more ideas does not meaningfully improve the probability that someone will come up with the optimal idea to satisfy unmet customer needs.** People are in effect brainstorming ideas without ever knowing what all the customer's needs are or which of those needs are unmet. We know that in any given market a customer has 50 to 150 needs (how we know this will be discussed later) and that anywhere from 5 to 80 percent of those needs may be unmet.

The mathematical probability of someone coming up with an idea that satisfactorily addresses all the customer's unmet needs without knowing what they are or whether or not they are satisfied is close to zero. *[Given the number of possible ways that just 15 unmet needs could be satisfied by products and services in any given market, millions of ideas would have to be generated before an exhaustive set of ideas could be created. If you assume three competing ideas for each of 15 unmet needs in various combinations, then you are generating ideas on the order of three to the power of 15, which is 14 million ideas. The chances of any one idea effectively addressing 15 unmet needs are one in 14 million. Furthermore, in most markets, we find there are more than 15 unmet needs.]*

Generating more ideas that fail to address unmet customer needs is misguided, and doing something bad faster does not lead to better results.

This approach to innovation is analogous to expecting a sharpshooter to hit a target without knowing what the target is. It is like expecting a doctor to recommend the right treatment without knowing what is wrong or what the symptoms are.

This brings us to a second reason why the ideas-first approach is doomed to failure: **the evaluation and filtering processes are flawed.**

Because the customer's unmet needs are unknown, the evaluation and filtering processes used today can easily miss great ideas and fail to filter out bad ideas. Let's remember what the evaluation and filtering process is supposed to do: separate the useful ideas from the useless ones. Or, in other words, choose the ideas that best address the customer's unmet needs. And yet, this evaluation and filtering process is typically executed without knowing what the customer's needs are.

Lacking explicit knowledge of customers' unmet needs, managers rely on intuition or evaluate proposed concepts using methods such as conjoint analysis, paired comparisons, and forced-choice scaling techniques, along with surveys and qualitative methods such as focus groups. These methods and others like them rely on customers to evaluate how well a proposed idea will address their unmet needs without truly understanding the product or technology and how it explicitly relates to those needs. Such an evaluation and filtering process is faulty in several respects. The first and most obvious one, mentioned earlier, is that chances are great that the best solution is not even in the consideration set. But there is also the fact that customers may not be able to make the connection between the technology and their needs. It is not surprising, then, that companies using the ideas-first approach to innovation struggle to achieve success rates greater than 10 to 20 percent.

The third reason why the ideas-first approach is doomed is that **customers cannot articulate the solutions they want.** In most cases, the customer is not a scientist, engineer, researcher or materials expert. They don't know what solutions are possible, but why should they?

The question I like to ask is, **"Why are we even asking customers what solutions they want?"**

Why should a company depend on the customer to know the best solution?

Why hire the customer to do the job of the marketing, development, and product planning team?

Coming up with the winning solution is not the customer's responsibility. It is the responsibility of the company.

THE NEEDS-FIRST APPROACH IS OFTEN FLAWED IN EXECUTION

Those who have recognized the inherent flaws in the ideas-first approach often attempt to follow a needs-first approach to innovation. Using this approach, companies first attempt to understand the customer's needs, and then figure out which are unmet and devise a concept that addresses those unmet needs.

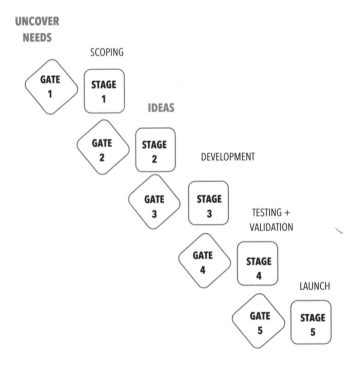

This thinking, though different from the ideas-first approach, is also supported by many academics, businesses, and suppliers.

Theodore Levitt, for example, in his 1960 landmark *Harvard Business Review* article, "Marketing Myopia," states, "An industry begins with the customer and his or her needs, not with a patent, a raw material, or a selling skill." *[Theodore Levitt, "Marketing Myopia," Harvard Business Review 38, no. 4 (July-August 1960).]*

Since then, others have drawn a similar conclusion.

Harvard Business School professor **David Garvin** has noted, "Studies comparing successful and unsuccessful innovation have found that the primary discriminator was the degree to which user needs were fully understood." *[David Garvin, A Note on Corporate Venturing and New Business Creation (Boston: Harvard Business School Press, 2002), 5.]*

In theory, if all the customer's unmet needs are known, then ideas can be generated to address them—and these ideas will have obvious value.

Over the years, many methods have been utilized to capture customer needs. These include focus groups, personal interviews, customer visits, and ethnographic, contextual, and observational research methods in addition to interviewing techniques such as voice of the customer (VOC), lead user analysis, and storytelling.

Despite the available needs-gathering methods, companies nearly always fail to uncover all or even most of the customer's needs.

How is this possible?

While nearly every manager agrees that the goal of innovation is to devise solutions that address unmet customer needs, **a common language for communicating a need does not exist.**

In research we conducted, we found that 95 percent of managers say there is internal disagreement on what a need is and how a need should be defined. Marketing and development teams in particular have strongly opposing views on what constitutes an actionable need statement. Consequently, while many employees may have customer knowledge, companies rarely have a complete list of agreed upon customer needs. Is there anyone in your organization that knows all the customer's needs? Is there agreement across the organization on what the customer's needs are? Is there agreement on which needs are unmet? If not, then how can there be agreement on what products and services to produce?

The sad reality is that despite all the talk about satisfying customer needs, **there is very little understanding of what characteristics a customer need statement**

should possess and what the structure, content, and syntax of a need statement should be.

Abbie Griffith and **John Hauser** loosely defined "customer need" in their 1991 article "Voice of the Customer" as "a description, in the customer's own words, of the benefit that he, she or they want fulfilled by the product or service." *[Abbie Griffin and John Hauser, "Voice of the Customer," Marketing Science 12, no. 1 (Winter 1993), 4.]*

Today we know that obtaining inputs in the customer's own words will more often than not result in the wrong inputs. Most managers, consultants, and academics agree that companies must look beyond the customer's own words to extract the kind of input that is needed, but they cannot seem to agree on whether or not a need is a description of customer benefit, a measure of customer value, a statement of a problem, or something else entirely.

We also find that managers cannot agree on how the statement should look, what information it should contain, how it should be grammatically structured, or what types of words and phrases should be used or avoided to ensure variability is not introduced into the statement—variability that can adversely affect later prioritization of unmet needs. Managers find themselves in a position that is analogous to that of a chef who knows that certain ingredients are required to produce a certain taste but is unable to figure out precisely what combination to use. And once forced into that position, getting it right becomes a process of trial and error.

Many academics, consultants, and supplier firms end up regarding the collection of these customer inputs as an art. In fact, some of the most popular approaches today utilize anthropologists to "seek out epiphanies through a sense of Vuja De," as IDEO general manager **Tom Kelley** says in *The Ten Faces of Innovation. [Tom Kelley makes that statement on page 17 of The Ten Faces of Innovation (New York: Doubleday, 2005).* He goes on to say that anthropologists have a half a dozen distinguishing characteristics that include, for example, practicing the Zen principle of "beginner's mind," embracing human behavior with all its surprises, and drawing inferences by listening to their intuition. Our opinion is that while this approach works for IDEO, it makes innovation more of an art than a science.

Others do not discriminate one type of input from another. For example, Gerry Katz, the vice president of Applied Marketing Science, Inc., writes, "[In distinguishing between needs and solutions] Ulwick adds the term desired outcomes... a useful description to be sure, just as Christensen has popularized the term jobs. But neither of these is conceptually any different from the other terms that have been in use since at least the mid-1980's: wants, needs, requirements, benefits, problem, tasks that the customer is trying to accomplish, and jobs which the customer is trying to get done."

All these terms are not conceptually the same. As we shall show, the nuanced differences between these terms, as revealed through Jobs-to-be-Done Theory, represent a breakthrough in innovation—one that can easily be overlooked when viewed through a traditional VoC lens.

To make matters worse, there is also a widely held assumption amongst company managers that customers have latent needs, or needs that customers are unable to articulate.

For 20 years, this belief has been supported and perpetuated by many well-respected individuals and organizations. In their 1991 best seller, *Competing for the Future*, **Gary Hamel** and **C. K. Prahalad** warn companies of the risk they run if they cannot get a view of the needs customers can't articulate.

The Product Development Management Association (PDMA) states that **"customer needs, either expressed or yet-to-be-articulated, provide new product development opportunities for the firm."** *[From the definition of "customer needs" in The PDMA Glossary for New Product Development (Mount Laurel, NJ: PDMA, 2006), http://www.pdma.org/npd_glossary.cfm.]*

Peter Sharzynski and **Rowan Gibson** explain in *Innovation to the Core* that "radical innovators are deeply empathetic; they understand—and feel—the unvoiced need of customers." *[Peter Skarzynski and Rowan Gibson, Innovation to the Core, 69.]*

Even the process-oriented P&G CEO, **A. G. Lafley**, says in The Game-Changer that "great innovations come from understanding the customer's unmet needs and desires, both articulated and unarticulated—that is, not only what they say, but, more important, what they cannot articulate or do not want to say." *[A. G. Lafley and Ram Charan, The Game-Changer (New York: Crown Business, 2008), 45.]*

As a result of this belief, **many companies assume that it is impossible to capture a complete set of customer need statements and that they have no choice but to execute the innovation process without knowing all of them.** But this conclusion is far from the truth.

As amazing as it sounds, the truth is companies routinely try to satisfy customers' needs without a clear definition of what a need even is. It is like trying to solve a word puzzle without knowing what a "word" is. So let's not assume customers have latent needs.

Why does it matter? Take a look at your organization. Everything it does is based on what unmet needs the company decides to target. The marketing team must know the customer's needs in order to define the company's value proposition, segment markets, position products and services, and create marketing communications. The development team must know the customer's needs so it can understand the strengths and weaknesses of the company's products, decide what new features to add to existing products and what new products to create. The R&D department makes technology investments based on its understanding of customer needs. Finally, the sales team's success depends on its ability to show customers that the company's products meet their needs.

How to get a handle on customer needs is an unsolved mystery—and that mystery is killing innovation. *Before a company can succeed at innovation, managers must agree on what a need is—and the types of needs that customers have.*

The key to solving this mystery lies in **Jobs-to-be-Done Theory.**

2.

JOBS-TO-BE-DONE NEEDS FRAMEWORK

Imagine the implications of knowing all your customer's needs. How many people in your organization today know all your customer's needs? Imagine if they all shared a common understanding of what a need is. How would decision-making improve if everybody in your organization had knowledge of all your customer's needs? How much more effective would your product and marketing teams be if it were possible to determine with a high level of confidence exactly what customer needs are underserved? What possibilities would arise if it became possible to discover segments of customers with unique sets of unmet needs? Knowledge of all the customer's needs changes everything. So how can it be achieved?

Harvard Business School marketing professor Theodore Levitt said, "People don't want to buy a quarter-inch drill. They want a quarter-inch hole!" Clayton Christensen said, "People buy products and services to get a job done". In his most recent book he says, "Customers don't buy products; they pull them into their life to make progress."

These are the basic constructs of Jobs-to-be-Done Theory, but these constructs are only the tip of the iceberg. Jobs-to-be-Done Theory has a game-changing implication:

Jobs-to-be-Done Theory provides a framework for (i) categorizing, defining, capturing, and organizing all your customer's needs, and (ii) tying customer-defined performance metrics (in the form of desired outcome statements) to the Job-to-be-Done.

Knowing all the customer's needs in a given market dramatically changes the way a company approaches the innovation process. With a complete set of customer needs in hand, a company is able to discover hidden segments of opportunity, determine which needs are underserved and overserved, decide which strategies to pursue, simplify ideation, test concepts for their ability to get a job done in advance of their development, and align the actions of marketing, development, and R&D to systematically create customer value.

With knowledge of all the customer's needs and which are unmet, a company can predict which new concepts and offerings will win in the marketplace. Evaluating a new concept against all the needs (when those needs are defined as the metrics customers use to measure value when getting a job done) will reveal how much better a proposed concept will get the job done.

Because customers are loyal to getting a job done, customers will switch to new solutions when they are able to get the job done significantly better. In our experience, new products that get the job done 20 percent better or more are very likely to win in the marketplace. Knowing that a product will get the job done 20 percent or more is the key to predictable innovation. ODI makes this possible.

While applying Jobs-to-be-Done Theory over the past 25 years, I have developed the **Jobs-to-be-Done Needs Framework** (see the figure on the next page).

This framework introduces the types of customer needs that must be considered to gain a deep understanding of what a customer is trying to accomplish. They include (i) the core functional Job-to-be-Done, (ii) the desired outcomes tied to the core functional Job-to-be-Done, (iii) related jobs, (iv) emotional and social jobs, (v) consumption chain jobs, and (vi) the buyer's financial desired outcomes.

While a job describes the overall task the customer is trying to execute, an outcome is a metric the customer uses to measure success and value while executing a job. For every functional and consumption chain job there exists a set of up to 50 or more desired outcome statements.

The **Jobs-to-be-Done Needs Framework** reveals the complexity involved in understanding all the needs in a market. It is not as if the customer has a handful of needs, or that there is just one customer. A diverse group of customers in a given market often collectively have well over 100 needs. In more complex markets such as health care and social media, customers may have 200 needs or more.

JOBS-TO-BE-DONE NEEDS FRAMEWORK

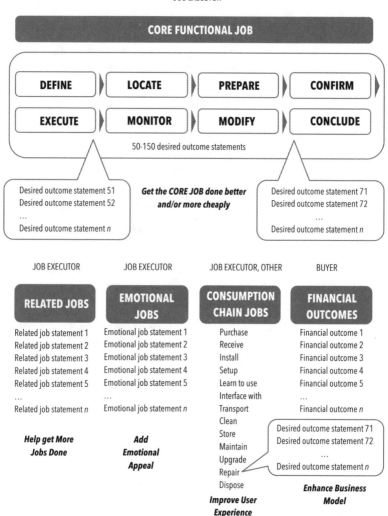

JOB EXECUTOR

CORE FUNCTIONAL JOB

| DEFINE | LOCATE | PREPARE | CONFIRM |
| EXECUTE | MONITOR | MODIFY | CONCLUDE |

50-150 desired outcome statements

Desired outcome statement 51
Desired outcome statement 52
...
Desired outcome statement *n*

Get the CORE JOB done better and/or more cheaply

Desired outcome statement 71
Desired outcome statement 72
...
Desired outcome statement *n*

| JOB EXECUTOR | JOB EXECUTOR | JOB EXECUTOR, OTHER | BUYER |

| **RELATED JOBS** | **EMOTIONAL JOBS** | **CONSUMPTION CHAIN JOBS** | **FINANCIAL OUTCOMES** |

Related job statement 1
Related job statement 2
Related job statement 3
Related job statement 4
Related job statement 5
...
Related job statement *n*

Emotional job statement 1
Emotional job statement 2
Emotional job statement 3
Emotional job statement 4
Emotional job statement 5
...
Emotional job statement *n*

Purchase
Receive
Install
Setup
Learn to use
Interface with
Transport
Clean
Store
Maintain
Upgrade
Repair
Dispose

Financial outcome 1
Financial outcome 2
Financial outcome 3
Financial outcome 4
Financial outcome 5
...
Financial outcome *n*

Desired outcome statement 71
Desired outcome statement 72
...
Desired outcome statement *n*

Help get More Jobs Done

Add Emotional Appeal

Improve User Experience

Enhance Business Model

The customers' needs are multilayered and complex. Customers have needs related to buying, using, and owning a product. They have emotional and functional needs. Customer need statements are mutually exclusive—they are defined independent of each other. A complete set of needs is collectively exhaustive—it incorporates all the needs a customer has for a given job. Each need must be stated separately and categorized correctly. Why?

The goal of innovation is to devise solutions that address unmet customer needs. For a company to be successful at innovation, this means it must not only know all the needs in the market, but it must be able to determine which needs are unmet. It must also be able to determine if there are segments of customers with different unmet needs. These are the insights that enable the innovation process to become more predictable. Without these insights innovation remains a game of chance. Having them changes everything.

What are the chances, for example, that a company will randomly conceptualize a solution that addresses 14 unmet needs in a segment of the market that represents about 25 percent of users? It's very unlikely to happen by chance. A company would have to know the segment exists and precisely what needs are underserved before it could predictably achieve success.

But how long would it take a product planning team to conceptualize a solution that addresses those same 14 unmet needs if they knew the segment existed and exactly what those unmet needs were? In the case of the Bosch circular saw product team (see the case study in chapter 5), it took just 3 hours. This is the power of the ODI process. Innovation is transformed from a game of chance to a science when the customer's desired outcomes (customer metrics) are known in advance of ideation.

One important factor that cannot be overlooked is that most markets are not homogeneous—meaning **in nearly every market, customers do not agree on what needs are unmet.** Some customers in nearly every market struggle more than others to get a job done. This confirms what we learned in marketing 101—in nearly every market exists segments of customers with unique sets of unmet needs.

Discovering segments of customers with unique sets of unmet needs and determining precisely what unmet needs exist in a segment requires statistically valid market research, not just observation or other qualitative research methods. Customer personas that are built around demographic and psychographic data and claim to represent customer "segments" are highly misleading as they usually create phantom targets.

Trying to guess at what needs-based segments exist and which needs are unmet introduces risk and variability into the innovation process. This is why statistically valid quantitative research is an essential part of the ODI process.

All of this begins with understanding what a need is and what type of needs customers have. The **Jobs-to-be-Done Needs Framework** provides an important function. Given all the customer insights that companies consider each day, the framework reveals what inputs are needed, how they should be categorized and organized, why they are captured, and how they should be used. The framework brings order to a historically chaotic practice.

THE CORE FUNCTIONAL JOB-TO-BE-DONE

People buy products and services to get a job done. The job the end user is trying to get done is the core functional job. A deep understanding of the core functional job enables a company to create product or service offerings that get the job done significantly better than competing solutions.

The core functional job is defined in a single statement, such as "cut a piece of wood in a straight line", "pass on life lessons to children", or "monitor a patient's vital signs". How a company should go about and define the core functional job is discussed in Chapter 4.

The core functional job is the anchor around which all other needs are defined. It is defined first, then the emotional, related and consumption chain jobs are defined relative to the core functional job. For example, if the core functional job were defined as "pass on life lessons to children", then we would seek to discover the customer's emotional and related jobs as they are trying to "pass on life lessons to children". All other jobs are in the context executing the core job.

Companies routinely want to know the functional jobs that customers are trying to get done for two reasons: (1) so they can discover new jobs to address (or new markets to target), and (2) to define a market they are already serving in a new way so they can use Jobs-to-be-Done Theory to discover how to serve it better. While the first activity requires a company to discover multiple functional jobs a customer is trying to get done, the latter requires a clear definition of just one functional job.

Market selection, the more complex scenario, is defined as the process of deciding what new markets a company should enter to establish attractive new revenue streams. To execute this process a company should first pick the customers (job executors) it would like to target and then determine all the functional jobs those customers are trying to get done. Next, through quantitative research, a company can determine which of those jobs are most important and least satisfied and will make the most attractive markets to target for growth. This exercise is critical for startups and established companies who are making investment decisions that will drive their growth.

While new market discovery is important, we usually find ourselves helping companies' better position their existing offerings and creating new products and services in core markets they have been entrenched in for years. So more often then not, we find ourselves trying to figure out the core functional job(s) an existing customer is trying to get done. While this is generally not too complicated, it can be when the offering is a platform-level solution.

More specifically, in an existing market where a company's offering has many applications or purposes, it is more difficult to determine the core functional job(s) the customer is trying to get done. In situations like that, we employ qualitative research methods to uncover all the reasons a customer may use the offering and then use quantitative research and factor analysis to group together like attributes and discover the core jobs customers are trying to get done. This approach has proven effective in banking (where banks are a solution that are used to get many jobs done) and social media, an industry where the top players offer platform-level solutions that are used for hundreds of purposes.

When defined correctly, a functional Job-to-be-Done has three unique and extremely valuable characteristics:

First, **a job is stable; it doesn't change over time.** It's the delivery vehicle or the technology that changes. Take the music industry, for example. Over the years people have used many products to help them "listen to music" (the Job-to-be-Done). This has included record players, tape and cassette players, compact disc players, MP3s and streaming services. Through this decades-long evolution of drastically changing technology platforms, the Job-to-be-Done has remained the same. The job is a stable focal point around which to create customer value.

Second, **a job has no geographical boundaries**. People who live in the USA, France, UK, Germany, South Korea, China, Russia, Brazil and Australia have many jobs in common that they are trying to get done. The solutions they use to get those jobs done may vary dramatically from geography to geography, but the jobs are the same. The degree to which the customer's desired outcomes are underserved may also vary by geography, depending on the solutions they use, but their collective set of desired outcomes are the same. Consequently, knowledge of the Job-to-be-Done in one geography can be leveraged globally.

Third, **a job is solution agnostic.** The Job-to-be-Done does not care if your company provides product, software, or service offerings. The job has no solution boundaries. This means that a deep understanding of the job will inform the creation of a solution that combines hardware, software and service components. It also informs a digitalization strategy—ways to use technology to get a job done better.

DESIRED OUTCOMES ON THE CORE FUNCTIONAL JOB

By focusing on the core functional job the customer is trying to execute and studying it as you would study a process, it becomes possible to uncover the metrics that customers use to measure success and value as they execute each step in that job. These metrics are included in specially formed need statements we call "desired outcomes" (see chapter 4).

While defining the functional job correctly is important, uncovering the customer's desired outcomes (the metrics they use to measure success when get the job done) is the real key to success at innovation.

To uncover the customer's desired outcomes, we dissect the core functional job into its component parts (job steps) using a job map. The job map becomes the framework from which to capture desired outcome statements.

Desired outcome statements explain precisely how customers measure success and value as they go through each step of the core functional job. They describe how it is possible to get the job done more quickly, predictably, efficiently and without waste. It is common to find that between 50 and 150 desired outcomes statements are applicable to the core functional job. For example, when trying to listen to music, a listener may want to "minimize the time it takes to get the songs in the desired order for listening", or "minimize the likelihood that the music sounds distorted at high volume".

We follow a strict set of rules when constructing desired outcome statements—for example, they are purposely designed and structured to be measurable, controllable, actionable, devoid of solutions, and stable over time. They are also structured so they can be prioritized for importance and satisfaction using statistically valid market research methods.

RELATED JOBS

While getting the core functional job done, it may be important to the end user to get other functional jobs done as well. Knowing what those related jobs are is important as it can lead to the creation of a platform-level solution that gets many jobs done. It is not uncommon to find that 5 to 20 related jobs might be on the mind of the end user.

While making a presentation, for example, a knowledge worker may want to emphasize a point projected on a screen, advance slides, time the presentation, or shut off the projector. Enabling the execution of all these related jobs done on a single platform describes how the telescopic pointer of years ago has evolved into today's wireless presenter device. Its value increased as it enabled the presenter to get more related jobs done.

EMOTIONAL AND SOCIAL JOBS

While getting the core functional job done, it may also be important to the end user to address important emotional and social jobs. Emotional jobs define how customers want to feel or avoid feeling as a result of executing the core functional job. Social jobs define how the customer wants to be perceived by others.

For example, a parent who is trying to pass on life lessons to children may want to "feel appreciated" (an emotional job) and "be perceived as a caring parent" (a social job).

Emotional and social job statements are used to help inform the decisions that lead to the creation of the value proposition and the effective marketing, positioning, and design of a product or service.

It is not uncommon to find that 5 to 25 emotional and social jobs may be on the mind of the end user when executing the core functional job.

CONSUMPTION CHAIN JOBS

Products have a lifecycle. After a product is purchased (which is a separate job), it must be received, installed and set-up. Then someone has to learn how to use it and interface with it. Someone may also have to transport, clean, store, maintain, upgrade, repair, and dispose of it. While people don't buy a product so they can clean, repair and dispose of it, a product that simplifies product consumption along one or more of these dimensions could differentiate itself in the marketplace. Dyson, for example, created the bagless system for collecting and disposing of dirt in a vacuum cleaner, making consumption more convenient.

Shirt makers, who have differentiated themselves through non-iron shirts, serve as another example.

The jobs along the product lifecycle are called consumption chain jobs. Each consumption chain job is comprised of its own distinct set of desired outcome statements. The purchase process itself can be considered a consumption chain job as customers must research, evaluate and transact the purchase. This "purchase job" is often worth analyzing to help improve the purchase process. We have completed extensive research with Harte Hanks doing exactly that, revealing significant opportunities for retailers to improve the way they sell their products to in-store consumers.

Other consumption chain jobs are also a possible focal point for product improvement and competitive differentiation. Helping bio-meds more easily sterilize a surgical tool, for example, may result in a point of differentiation. Consumption chain jobs impact the customer journey and experience. Understanding the desired outcomes associated with relevant consumption chain jobs gives designers and engineers the information they need to be proficient at design-centered innovation. These inputs are an important ingredient in the recipe for innovation.

FINANCIAL DESIRED OUTCOMES

When buying a product or service, the purchase decision maker (buyer) uses a set of financial metrics to decide whether or not to buy product A or product B, or to buy from supplier A or supplier B. An understanding of the buyer's financial needs informs the decisions that lead to product and business model innovation. It is not uncommon to find that buyers consider 40 to 80 financial outcomes (metrics) when making the purchase decision. A hospital administrator who is responsible for buying medical devices, for example, may be looking for products that "reduce the patient's length of stay", or "reduce morbidity rates". These metrics have cost implications that drive the purchase decision.

In the case where the buyer is also the user, it is important to make sure the buyer is wearing the buyer's hat when describing the financial metrics used when making the purchase decision. Otherwise outcome statements regarding the core functional job may uncovered instead.

Jobs-to-be-Done Theory unlocks the mystery that has for decades been clouding the understanding of customer needs. Knowing how to classify all the customer's needs changes everything.

3.

THE JOBS-TO-BE-DONE GROWTH STRATEGY MATRIX

Once a company knows all the customer's needs, which of those needs are underserved and overserved, and what unique under-and overserved segments of customers exist, it must decide if and how it will target each segment. For example, managers would want to determine if they should (i) add a new feature set to its existing offering, (ii) develop a new low cost offering, (iii) create a new platform-level solution that gets the job done significantly better, or do something else entirely.

A company must decide what strategy should be pursued to ensure it wins in the marketplace.

Over the course of many client engagements, we have employed Jobs-to-be-Done Theory to help create a strategy framework that (i) explains what causes new product and service offerings to win or fail in the marketplace, and (ii) helps to select the growth strategy that fits the situation and will ensure a win in the marketplace.

When we use Jobs-to-be-Done Theory to examine product successes and failures, we observe the same phenomenon time and time again: **new products and services win in the marketplace if they help customers get a job done better (faster, more predictably, with higher output) and/or more cheaply.**

This simple observation led us to the effective classification of five unique growth strategies companies can adopt in the quest to win in a market. It also resulted in the creation of the **Job-to-be-Done Growth Strategy Matrix**, a framework that illustrates when and how these strategies should be used. With this framework, companies can understand past successes and failures and can adopt a strategy to create winning products and services in the future.

ESTABLISHING THE THEORY

Having recognized that new products and services win when they get a job done better and/or more cheaply, we set out to transform this insight into a predictive framework for growth. We began by "**categorizing the possibilities**" using the matrix shown.

The matrix suggests that companies can create products and services that are (1) better and more expensive, (2) better and less expensive, (3) worse and less expensive, and (4) worse and more expensive.

	Charge **MORE**	Charge **LESS**
Get JOB DONE **BETTER**	**BETTER** + More EXPENSIVE	**BETTER** + Less EXPENSIVE
Get JOB DONE **WORSE**	**WORSE** + More EXPENSIVE	**WORSE** + Less EXPENSIVE

The matrix prompted us to ask what types of customers might be targeted with a product or service offering in each quadrant. Our experience and the work of others in this field led us to the following five conclusions regarding the four quadrants:

1. A better-performing, more expensive product will only appeal to underserved customers. These are customers who have unmet needs and are willing to pay more to get a job done better.

2. A better-performing, less expensive product will appeal to all customers.

3. A worse-performing, less expensive product will appeal to overserved customers (those with no unmet needs). It will also appeal to nonconsumers. These are people whose current solutions don't involve the market at all, or who are not even attempting to get the job done as they cannot afford any of the existing solutions.

4. A worse-performing, more expensive product will only appeal to customers for whom limited (or no) alternatives are available. This happens in unique or atypical situations.

5. Some products are "stuck in the middle" (to borrow a term from Michael Porter): they only get a job done slightly better or slightly cheaper. Such a product will likely fail to attract any new customers. This is clearly a poor strategy for a new market entrant, but it may help an incumbent company retain existing customers.

Next, we place the customers in their respective quadrants, highlighting the differences in target customer-type:

	Charge **MORE**	Charge **LESS**
Get JOB DONE **BETTER**	**Win underserved customers**	**Win all types of customers** (under - overserved)
Get JOB DONE **WORSE**	**Win customers with limited options**	**Win overserved customers**

THE JOBS-TO-BE-DONE GROWTH STRATEGY MATRIX

We concluded that each of the five situations warrant its own distinct strategy. With the goal of creating a framework for proactive strategy formulation, we asked, **"What unique strategy can be employed in each of these five situations?"**

We set out to define and name a type of strategy that would work for each unique situation. We chose a naming convention that built upon well-established strategy and innovation terminology and accurately described the uniqueness of the situation.

The five strategies we identified address all the situations a company can face as it contemplates a product or service strategy. The strategies are introduced in the **Jobs-to-be-Done Growth Strategy Matrix** shown below:

The product/service strategies introduced in this framework are defined as follows:

- **Differentiated strategy.** A company pursues a differentiated strategy when it discovers and targets a population of underserved consumers with a new product or service offering that gets a job (or multiple jobs) done significantly better, but at a significantly higher price. Examples of offerings that successfully employed a differentiated strategy include Nest's thermostat, Nespresso's coffee and espresso machines, Apple's iPhone 2G, the Herman Miller Aeron chair, Whole Foods' organic food products, Emirates airlines' international flights, Bang & Olufsen's personal audio products, BMW sports cars, Sony's PlayStation (original model), and the Dyson vacuum cleaner and Airblade hand dryer.

- **Dominant strategy.** A company pursues a dominant strategy when it targets all consumers in a market with a new product or service offering that gets a job done significantly better and for significantly less money. Examples of offerings that successfully employed a dominant strategy include Google Search, Google AdWords, UberX, Netflix's streaming video, Progressive Insurance's nonstandard automobile insurance, and Vanguard Group's personal investment services.

- **Disruptive strategy.** A company pursues a disruptive strategy when it discovers and targets a population of overserved customers or nonconsumers with a new product or service offering that enables them to get a job done more cheaply, but not as well as competing solutions. Examples of offerings that successfully employed a disruptive strategy include Google Docs (relative to Microsoft Office), TurboTax (relative to traditional tax services), Dollar Shave Club's razor offering (relative to Gillette), eTrade's online trading platform (relative to traditional financial brokerages) and Coursera's online educational services (relative to traditional universities).

- **Discrete strategy.** A company pursues a discrete strategy when it targets a population of "restricted" customers with a product that gets the job done worse, yet costs more. This strategy can work in situations where customers are legally, physically, emotionally, or otherwise restricted in how they can get a job done. Examples of offerings that successfully employ a discrete strategy include drinks sold in airports past security checkpoints, stadium concessions at sporting events, check-cashing and payday-lending services, and ATMs in remote locations.

- **Sustaining strategy.** A company pursues a sustaining strategy when it introduces a new product or service offering that gets the job done only slightly better and/or slightly cheaper. Examples of offerings that successfully employ a sustaining strategy are plentiful.

A company may have many products and services in one market, each employing different strategies, as defined above. For that reason, it is important to source examples at the product level, not at the company level.

Uber, for example, has offerings that make use of three of the strategies: UberBLACK employs a differentiated strategy, while UberPOOL employs a disruptive strategy (see figure below). The importance of this distinction becomes obvious when we begin to apply the model to predict the success or failure of a new product or service:

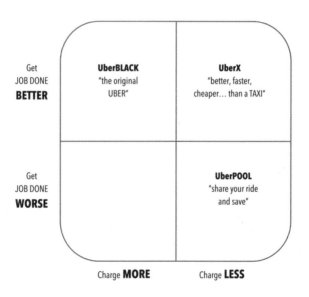

EMPLOYING THE FIVE GROWTH STRATEGIES

The **Job-to-be-Done Growth Strategy Matrix** can be used to prescribe proactive short- and long-term strategies for success, but to use it, a company must know whether or not there are underserved and/or overserved segments of customers in the target market. Without this knowledge, there is no way to know which strategy to adopt, and the chances of picking the wrong one are high. For example, in an overserved segment, a differentiated strategy would likely fail, as no customer is seeking a more expensive product or service that will get the job done better. Conversely, in an underserved segment, a disruptive strategy would likely fail, as no customer is seeking a cheaper product or service that would get the job done worse.

The most effective way to discover whether or not there is an under-or overserved population is to segment a market around a complete set of prioritized customer desired outcome statements.

Our **Outcome-Based Segmentation™** methodology, which has always been part of our ODI process, was specifically designed for this purpose (see chapter 4).

Once a company knows where in the matrix its target customers can be found, it can adopt the appropriate strategies for each segment. Let us examine each strategy more closely.

Employing a Differentiated Strategy

A differentiated strategy works when a highly underserved segment of customers is targeted with a premium-priced offering that gets the job done significantly better. This strategy results in a disproportionate share of profits and is the strategy pursued by many of the world's fastest-growing and most profitable companies.

Nest, for example, a recent entrant into the home thermostat market, beat Honeywell, White-Rodgers, and other well-established incumbent firms with a product that was targeted at a highly underserved segment of the market, superior in performance, and offered at seven times the price of competing solutions ($250 versus $35). While capturing less than 10% market share, Nest is estimated to have captured over 25% profit share while shaking up the industry and putting its competitors on the defensive.

A differentiated strategy is attractive because it enables a company to enter a market at the high end, capture significant profit share, and work its way down market over time to gain additional market share. This is a way to move from employing a differentiated strategy with an initial product entry to employing a dominant strategy with other products over time. A company can successfully move down market by lowering the price of its older products as it introduces newer and better products into its portfolio, as Apple did with the series of iPhone product offerings, and/or by using operational innovation as a means to lower production costs, as Uber did when it employed freelance drivers to supply rides in its UberX offering.

Incumbents have much to gain by pursuing a differentiated strategy as they can afford to target their existing products at well-served or even overserved customers once their new, high-profit products are introduced. This puts the incumbent in a position of both profit and market share growth.

Employing a Dominant Strategy

A dominant strategy is always the most appealing approach for a new market entrant to take because incumbents cannot defend against it. Our experience suggests that companies can win with a dominant strategy if they introduce a product or service that gets the job done (addresses the customer's unmet desired outcomes) at least 20% better and at least 20% more cheaply. This can be measured with high precision and probability when evaluating a proposed concept against a complete set of desired outcome statements.

Netflix's streaming services, for example, offered greater convenience than traditional rental stores such as Blockbuster by making it easier to find, obtain, and consume movies. In addition, they reduced the cost of watching a movie by eliminating the annoying late-return fees and enabling customers to watch more content for a low monthly subscription rate.

We helped Kroll Ontrack enter the electronic evidence discovery market with a dominant strategy. While traditional competitors in this field gathered evidence manually, Kroll Ontrack created a solution that enabled legal teams to get the job done significantly better and more cheaply through the use of digital technology. This strategy led them to immediate success and market leadership that they have sustained for over a decade.

In any market, an incumbent or a new market entrant can win with a product or service that gets the job done significantly better and more cheaply. Incumbents are less likely to create such a product or service because it could dramatically cut their margins and may require an investment in a new product platform, capabilities, and resources.

Employing a Disruptive Strategy

The **Jobs-to-be-Done Growth Strategy Matrix** confirms that **Clayton Christensen**, who coined the term **disruptive innovation**, was correct: companies can win in overserved segments with products that enable customers to get a job done more cheaply, but not as well as competing solutions. Based on our model, we also agree with Christensen that a disruptive strategy successfully serves two customer segments: highly overserved customers (like users of Microsoft Word who switched to Google Docs) and nonconsumers—people who do not buy currently available products.

A disruptive strategy works in both situations, but for different reasons. It works for current consumers who are overserved, as Christensen's theory suggests, and are willing to make some sacrifices to get the job done more cheaply. Nonconsumers, on the other hand, are underserved: they simply can't afford any of the solutions that are currently available. If a product comes along that they can afford, it will allow them to get the job done better than they can currently.

Christensen also correctly identified another phenomenon that occurs in the marketplace when he described **disruptive innovation** as "a process by which a product or service takes root initially in simple applications at the bottom of a market and then relentlessly moves up market, eventually displacing established competitors." Seen through the Job-to-be-Done lens, the "process of disruption" is best described as the introduction of a series of products, the first of which employs a disruptive strategy that gets the job done worse and more cheaply, followed by a series of products that build on that technology platform, with more and more features, until the newest offerings get the job done better and more cheaply (figure on next page).

Although a new market entrant is more likely to pursue a disruptive strategy, incumbents have an equal or better chance at winning with a disruptive offering if they pursue it. The problem for many companies is that it is often a less profitable strategy. Proponents have to convince management that it will defend against competitors and new market entrants. Since a company is not limited to one product, it can choose, as Uber did, to create separate products to address over-and underserved customer segments.

Employing a Discrete Strategy

A discrete strategy is employed as a separate (discrete) part of an existing product strategy: with a discrete strategy, a company takes an existing product and sells it in a unique situation that justifies a higher price. A discrete strategy is best suited for situations in which a higher-priced version of the existing product would be very welcome—or where a captive clientele cannot object. Pursuing a discrete strategy can be very profitable.

The key to a successful discrete strategy is the ability to identify situations in which the customer, in need of the company's product, has restricted or no access to it. In such a situation, the company can justify charging a higher price for its purchase. For example, people who are unable to cash a check at a bank because they do not have a bank account have no choice but to pay high fees to cash their checks at an independent check-cashing center. Stubhub.com also capitalizes on this scarcity strategy by allowing tickets that are sold out to be re-sold/auctioned to people for what the market will pay, often at much higher-than-normal prices.

As another example, consider airline travelers who are legally prohibited from taking bottles of drinking water through security. This restriction enables concessions at the gates to employ a discrete strategy, as they are now justified in charging significantly more for water (and many other food and beverage items) to travelers. Similarly, movie theaters, sporting arenas, and theme parks restrict what visitors can bring in and consequently are able to employ a similar strategy.

Restrictions resulting from high demand can also justify higher prices. Airlines, for example, typically charge more for seats when supply is tight. It should be noted that although employing a discrete strategy may hold the potential for high profits, it can also be viewed as exploitative by customers and result in public backlash and/or reputational damage as it has with pharmaceutical giant Mylan over the high cost of EpiPens.

Employing a Sustaining Strategy

A sustaining strategy is good for products or services that get the job done just slightly better and/or more cheaply. We define "slightly" as less than 5% better or cheaper. New market entrants should avoid a sustaining strategy, as they will not be offering anything enticing enough to lure customers away en masse from a favorite brand or product. The risk is too high to make a switch. Customers generally will only switch to a new product if it gets the job done upwards of 20% better—which is characteristic of a differentiated or dominant strategy. Here again, using desired outcome statements as the basis for evaluating whether or not a product will get the job done better (and how much better) is a critical step in bringing data-driven decision making to the innovation process.

Sustaining innovation is a good strategy for an incumbent to follow to maintain market position, market share, and margins. In established markets, getting the job done slightly better and slightly more cheaply lets a company take share from a competitor.

The Jobs-to-be-Done Growth Strategy Matrix reveals which growth strategies are available for a company to pursue in a given situation.

As I shall show in the next chapter, the qualitative and quantitative research methods included in **the Outcome-Driven Innovation process secure the information that is needed to determine what situation a company is in.**

Once a company knows what under- or overserved segments exist and what customer needs are under- and overserved, it is in a position to use the matrix to select the best strategy for pursuit. Without this ability, innovation remains a game of chance.

PROCESS

4.

OUTCOME DRIVEN-INNOVATION

A company's success at innovation is dependent on the innovation process it choses to employ. A process fraught with defects and deficiencies will produce unpredictable results.

When it comes to creating an effective innovation process, cobbling together a hodgepodge of incompatible practices and relying on qualitative insights alone just doesn't work. What companies need is a comprehensive, customer-centric, data-driven innovation process that is built around Jobs Theory. That is why the Strategyn team and I have spent the last 25 years creating and refining our **Outcome-Driven Innovation (ODI)** process. ODI rids the innovation process of its deficiencies.

While **Jobs-to-be-Done** is the **theory, Outcome-Driven Innovation** is the **process** that puts it into **practice**.

ODI is a strategy and innovation process that enables companies to conceptualize and invent new solutions that help customers get a job done better and/or more cheaply. It has an 86 percent success rate because it begins with a deep understanding of the Job-to-be-Done and employs unique quantitative research methods that enable companies to analyze markets in ways that have never before been possible.

More specifically, **ODI links a company's value creation activities to customer-defined performance metrics related to the job they are trying to get done**—a truly revolutionary concept in the field.

By supplying a definition of customer needs that the entire organization can embrace, ODI offers a rigorous, controlled approach to needs gathering, needs-based segmentation, competitive analysis, opportunity identification, idea generation and validation, market sizing, and the formulation of market and product strategy. The result is a predictable approach to innovation.

As shown in the figure, the **Outcome-Driven Innovation** process is comprised of 10 key steps.

I. Define the Customer

II. Define the Jobs-to-be-Done

III. Uncover Customer Needs

IV. Find Segments of Opportunity

V. Define the Value Proposition

VI. Conduct the Competitive Analysis

VII. Formulate the Innovation Strategy

VIII. Target Hidden Growth Opportunities

IX. Formulate the Market Strategy

X. Formulate the Product Strategy

The ODI process begins with a definition of the customer and ends with a market and product strategy that creates value for that customer.

This chapter outlines the process we use and the steps that we take to turn Jobs Theory into practice.

I. DEFINE THE CUSTOMER

Before a company can understand the customer's needs, company managers must agree on exactly who the customer is.

Gaining such agreement is not easy. When we ask company managers who their customer is, we typically hear, "We have many customers." Often they add that customers include both "internal stakeholders and external customers." To further complicate matters, external customers are typically said to include influencers, decision makers, buying groups, end users, operators, installers, and others. In a medical device company, for example, external customers include the surgeon, patient, insurer, nurse, operating-room manager, and hospital buying group, among others. It's true that a company has many customers, but is there a way to simplify matters?

Let's start with the why question. **Why do we need to know who the customer is?** Obviously, we want to know whom it is we're trying to serve, but there is a more tactical reason. From a strategy and innovation perspective, we must identify the customer so we can gain the insights we need to create products and services that will get the job done better and/or more cheaply.

So the question becomes, **"Who holds these insights?"** Through our work, we have discovered that there are three key customers types (or job executors) that must be considered: the end user (or functional job executor), the product life cycle support team, and the purchase decision maker.

THE END USER

The end user is the person who uses the product or service to get the core functional job done. In many situations, the end user and the purchase decision maker are different people. The end user can provide your company with the functional metrics (desired outcomes) it needs to figure out how to create a product that will get the job done faster, more predictably, and more efficiently, with higher output or throughput.

For a medical device manufacturer, the end user of a surgical tool is the surgeon. The surgeon may be seeking products or services that will "minimize the likelihood of removing healthy tissue" or "quickly determine the points of affixation for attachment." End users are also able to provide your company with a list of their emotional jobs and their related jobs, two other key inputs identified in the Jobs-to-be-Done Needs Framework

THE PRODUCT LIFE CYCLE SUPPORT TEAM

The product lifecycle support team is comprised of the people who install, set up, store, transport, maintain, repair, clean, upgrade, and dispose of the product. In certain situations, the end user may also be part of product life cycle support team. Not all these consumption chain jobs apply in every situation, but the people responsible for the ones that do apply can provide your company with the desired outcome statements that will lead to a product that requires less support.

A product that does not have to be installed, set up, stored, transported, and so on, is far more valuable than one that does. Simplifying or eliminating these consumption chain jobs has two key benefits: (i) it can lower the cost of product ownership, which satisfies the needs of the purchase decision maker, and (ii) it makes the product more convenient to use, which satisfies the needs of the end user. All those responsible for supporting the product throughout its lifecycle are key customers because their insights make it possible for the company to create a more positive customer experience.

THE PURCHASE DECISION MAKER

The purchase decision maker is responsible for seeking out and evaluating alternative offerings and deciding which to buy. The purchase decision maker can provide your company with the financial desired outcomes it needs to figure out how to create a product or service that will get the job done more cheaply. The buyer of a surgical tool (who could be an operating-room manager, a hospital administrator, or someone holding another title), for example, may be seeking products that will "reduce the patient's length of stay" or "reduce the likelihood of a recurrence." Financial metrics such as these drive the buying decision.

By focusing on these three customers, a company will gain the insights it needs to create a product or service that will get a job done better along multiple dimensions—and more cheaply. More importantly, if your company creates a product or service that addresses the unmet needs of all three of these customers, it will find that influencers will recommend it, distributors and retailers will carry it, those on social media will promote it, people will buy it, and your internal stakeholders will be satisfied by the financial rewards.

II. DEFINE THE JOB-TO-BE-DONE

Making the core functional job the unit of analysis is the cornerstone of successful innovation. The core functional job is the stable, long-term focal point around which all other needs are defined and around which value creation should be centered.

Defining the core functional Job-to-be-Done correctly is a prerequisite to predictable success.

Getting it wrong is a big problem, and getting it right is not that easy. Defining the job too narrowly will limit the discovery of growth opportunities. Defining the job too broadly will result in non-actionable insights.

From our experience, most products only get part of a job done. The goal is to discover the entire job the customer is trying to accomplish. This is why it is incorrect to ask a customer, "What job did you hire that product to do?" as this may not reveal the entire job. Asking this question is a common mistake. It is indicative of a product-centric mindset.

To avoid defining the job to narrowly, work directly with customers to understand not why they bought your product, but how your product fits into what they are trying to accomplish. Ask, "Why are you using that product, what job are you ultimately trying to get done".

For example, if a stove-top kettle maker were to ask its users "what job did you hire that product to do", it is likely they would tell you they hired it to "boil water". That may be correct, but boiling water is just a step in the job the customer is ultimately trying to get done—which is to "prepare a hot beverage for consumption". If the stove top kettle maker defines the job too narrowly, then it is at risk of a competitor coming along (like Keurig) with a solution that gets the entire job done on a single platform.

It is not uncommon for a new competitor to overtake a market by finding the capabilities, resources, funding, technology, and know how to create an offering that gets the entire job done.

On the other hand, defining the job too broadly can make it difficult, if not impossible, for the company to tackle the job in its entirety. To avoid this from happening, think about the company, its products and its capabilities and ask, "Can and will the company address this job from beginning to end over time?" If the company does not have or is not willing to acquire the capabilities, resources, funding, and technology and know how to tackle the broader job then the job is defined too broadly from a practical standpoint.

Take the customer's perspective: When defining the core functional job, think about the job from the customer's perspective, not the company's. For example, a company that supplies herbicides to farmers may conclude that growers are trying to "kill weeds," while the growers might say the Job-to-be-Done is to "prevent weeds from impacting crop yields."

Don't overcomplicate it: While the Jobs-to-be-Done Needs Framework is multilayered and complex, a functional job statement is not. It is important to emphasize that a well-defined functional job statement, and all the need statements we describe, are one-dimensional and mutually exclusive. Cramming everything into one complicated statement or a "job story" makes it impossible to later quantify exactly where the customer is underserved. The goal is to separately define all the causal factors that contribute variability to getting the job done. This is accomplished through 100 or more separate statements, not just one.

Leave emotion and other needs out of it: When defining the core functional job make sure it is defined as a functional job, not as a hybrid functional/emotional/social job. A functional job does not have social and emotional dimensions. The emotional and social jobs related to the core functional job are defined in a series of separate emotional job statements.

Also do not include desired outcomes in the functional job statement. They too must be stated separately. So if the job is to "cut a piece of wood in a straight line", don't say "accurately, safely and quickly cut a piece of wood in a straight line". Accurately, safely and quickly vaguely describe outcomes associated with getting the job done. A statement like "stay awake and occupied while I make my morning commute more fun" also fails this test. Here the functional job may be more like, "stay awake during my morning commute". A possible solution may be a good shot of espresso, but probably not a milkshake.

Define the job, not the situation: Do not define the Job-to-be-Done as a situation that a customer finds himself or herself in. Rather define the job around what the customer decides to do in that situation. For example, commuters may find themselves "on a long, boring commute", but "having a long and boring ride to work" is not a job—it is a situation commuters find themselves in. You cannot study the job of "overcoming boredom" because it is not a functional job.

Rather, consider what commuters choose to do when they are on a long, boring commute. What they may do is stop at a quick service restaurant to "get breakfast while commuting to work" (the actual functional Job-to-be-Done).

Similarly, you may find yourself bored waiting in line at a doctor's office, but again, overcoming boredom is not the job, nor is the job to "fill my time while waiting". Rather, what the customer chooses to do when she/he is bored is the real Job-to-be-Done. For example, when you are standing there in line waiting to see the doctor, you may choose to use your smartphone to "stay informed on topics of interest", "check your credit score", "pay bills", or execute other jobs that can be accomplished through a smartphone application. They are the Jobs-to-be-Done.

Define the job statement in the correct format: A job statement always begins with a verb and is followed by the object of the verb (a noun). The statement should also include a contextual clarifier. In the job statement "listen to music while on the go", the contextual clarification is made by adding "while on the go" to the job statement. Commuters who stop at quick service restaurant on the way to work are trying to "get breakfast while commuting to work" where "while commuting to work" brings needed context to the statement. Keep this format in mind:

Job statement = verb + object of the verb (noun) + contextual clarifier

III. UNCOVER CUSTOMER DESIRED OUTCOMES

With the core functional job defined, the next step in the ODI process is to create a "job map" for that job. A job map is a visual depiction of the core functional job, deconstructed into its discrete process or job steps, which explains in detail exactly what the customer is trying to get done. A job map does not show what the customer is doing (a solution view); rather, it describes what the customer is trying to get done (a needs view).

A job map is focused on the underlying goals of the actions being taken. For example, you wouldn't say an anesthesiologist is "looking at the display" (a solution that describes what action the anesthesiologist is taking). Instead, you would say the anesthesiologist is "monitoring the patient's vital signs", which is the underlying goal of looking at the display.

In addition, a job map is not a customer journey or customer experience map: it does not describe the journey the customer goes through to buy, receive, set-up, use, upgrade, clean and maintain a product. These activities are consumption chain jobs that are captured and treated separately. If you are focusing on the customer journey, you are not focused on the core functional job.

A good job map will describe what the customer is trying to get done independent of all the competing solutions that customers are using. In other words, it will be accurate for all customer situations, regardless of the products they are using to get the job done. A completed job map represents the "ideal process flow" for that job: all the steps in the ideal order for efficient execution.

We create the job map for a number of reasons:

- The completed job map lays out the long term strategy for the organization—which is to devise a solution that gets the entire job done on a single platform or with a single offering (which may include hardware, software and services).
- It is often the case that innovative ideas can come from analyzing the job map, as it points out holes and inefficiencies in existing offerings.
- From a tactical standpoint, the job map serves as a framework and a guide for capturing the customer's desired outcomes. For this reason, it is best to create the job map before attempting to capture desired outcome statements.

THE UNIVERSAL JOB MAP

Analysis of hundreds of jobs has revealed that all jobs consist of some or all of the eight fundamental process steps: define, locate, prepare, confirm, execute, monitor, modify and conclude (see the universal job map). This insight is essential for creating a framework around which customer needs (desired outcomes) are gathered. (To learn more about job mapping, see "The Customer-Centered Innovation Map" in the May 2008 issue of the Harvard Business Review.)

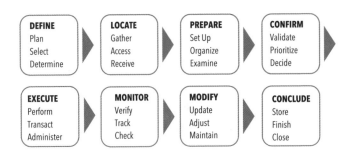

Once a job map is created for a specific functional job, desired outcomes are captured for each step in the job map. **For any given Job-to-be-Done, we often uncover between 50 and 150 desired outcome statements.**

Customers know perfectly well how they measure success when executing a job and are very capable of communicating those metrics—and those metrics, simply put, are their desired outcomes. A corn farmer, for example, may want to "minimize the time it takes for the corn seeds to germinate" or to "minimize the likelihood that the plants fail to emerge at the same time."

THE DESIRED OUTCOME STATEMENT

Desired-outcome statements must conform to a specific structure and follow a set of stringent rules. This is necessary because differences in structure, terminology, and syntax from statement to statement can introduce unwanted sources of variability that alter the importance and satisfaction ratings customers give the statements. This in turn will affect the way customers end up prioritizing innovation opportunities.

A desired outcome statement includes a direction of improvement, a performance metric (usually time or likelihood), an object of control (the desired outcome), and a contextual clarifier (describing the context in which the outcome is desired).

"Minimize the likelihood that the music sounds distorted when played at high volume" is one example of an outcome statement related to the job of listening to music.

When creating a desired outcome statement, remember the following structure:

Outcome statement = direction of improvement + performance metric + object of control + contextual clarifier

(See "Giving Customers a Fair Hearing," in the Spring 2008 issue of the *Sloan Management Review* for additional details on what a need is and the rules to follow when documenting outcome statements.)

Desired outcome statements can be uncovered using any of the popular interviewing methods, such as personal interviews, focus groups, or observational or ethnographic interviews.

While most qualitative research has a short shelf life, a complete set of desired outcome statements is an important company asset for years to come as desired outcomes don't change over time—the solutions that address them do.

With a complete set of desired outcome statements in hand, a company can gain quantitative insights into its market that were never before possible.

IV. FIND SEGMENTS OF OPPORTUNITY

Market segmentation is a method that companies use to target unique offerings to groups of customers that will value them. Over the years, many methods of market segmentation have been developed and implemented.

Qualitative methods, including the creation of personas, are used to segment markets using demographic, psychographic, or behavioral categories or stereotypes. Quantitative methods, such as conjoint analysis, aim for greater precision through the use of numerical values and calculations. Unfortunately, nearly all segmentation methods, whether qualitative or quantitative, fail to distinguish between customers with different unmet needs, which is the only form of segmentation that will deliver real value.

We have conducted hundreds of segmentation studies for companies in dozens of industries and have concluded that the differences in people's needs do not come from different demographics or psychographics. In fact, we have proven that demographic, psychographic, and behavioral and attitudinal data will nearly always fail to explain why customers have different unmet needs. A 28-year-old man from Montana with a college degree can have the same unmet needs as a 55-year-old woman from Florida who dropped out of high school. Both, for example, may be unhappy with their Internet service.

The only way to discover segments of customers with unique sets of unmet needs is to segment the market around unmet needs.

Until now this has not been possible as customer need statements designed for this purpose had not yet been invented. Desired outcome statements defined around the core functional job make effective needs-based possible.

Customers have different unmet needs because subsets of customers often encounter added difficulties that the other customers do not face. These added difficulties create additional unmet needs for that user. For example, in work we completed for Bosch, we discovered that some tradesmen who use circular saws to "cut wood in a straight line" (the Job-to-be-Done) had to make more finish cuts (for instance, to fit crown molding in a corner) than others. This means they had to make more blade height and angle adjustments. Because they encountered these additional complexities, they had unmet needs that other tradesmen did not have.

In work that we completed with an automotive company, we discovered that some drivers who were trying to "reach a destination on time" (the Job-to-be-Done) struggled more than others because they had to go to multiple locations during the day, rather than simply to the one destination. Because they had to go to many places, they encountered many different traffic patterns and associated problems (backed up traffic, parking difficulties, etc.). These added complexities made predicting travel time (to accomplish the Job-to-be-Done) much more difficult. In other words, this group had unmet needs that other drivers did not have.

In nearly all the markets we have analyzed, some segments of customers struggle more than others to get a job done. We argue that this presents a unique opportunity—but to seize it, companies must segment the market using unmet needs (which we capture in desired outcome statements), and not demographic, psychographic, or behavioral data. Our

Outcome-Based Segmentation methodology is executed in four steps:

- First we analyze the Job-to-be-Done and capture all the customers' needs in the form of desired outcome statements. (The special syntax of these outcome statements guarantees precision and comparability).
- Next, we field a survey that is administered to a statistically valid representative sample of customers (usually between 180 and 3,000 customers). Their answers reveal how important it is that they achieve each outcome and how well the solution they use today satisfies each outcome. With this data we determine which outcomes are most under-and overserved. Under-and overserved outcomes represent innovation opportunities.
- Third, we use factor analysis and cluster analysis to segment the market into groups of customers with unique sets of unmet desired outcomes.
- Lastly, we use profiling questions we include in the survey to understand what factors cause complexity and make some customers struggle more than others to get the job done. The survey also collects information that reveals the degree to which the different segments we uncovered are underserved.

Why does all this matter?

If you do not know what underserved segments and desired outcomes exist, you will not know which growth strategy to pursue. You will be guessing at innovation and competing on luck. Knowing if and why segments of customers have different unmet needs is the key to an effective market and product strategy. A new product will fail if it doesn't address unmet needs in a segment of the market that is large enough to warrant the investment. A value proposition will fail to connect with customers if it does not align with unmet customer needs.

When we conduct segmentation analysis, we find segments of customers that are underserved (they have unmet needs), overserved (they're getting extraneous features, perks, or services they don't value), and appropriately served (all their needs are satisfied without any extraneous features). One market may be composed of three underserved segments, while another market may comprise three overserved segments. A disruptive strategy in the former case would fail, as no segment of the market is overserved. A differentiated strategy in the latter case would fail as no segment of the market is underserved.

Because no market is homogeneous, outcome-based market segmentation is an essential ingredient in the formulation of market and product strategy. The key is to discover meaningful segments—hidden segments that offer the opportunity for value creation.

V. DEFINE THE VALUE PROPOSITION

A number of years ago we worked with Coloplast's wound care product team. More specifically, we focused on wound care nurses (the end users) whose Job-to-be-Done was "treat a wound." We used our **Outcome-Based Segmentation** methodology to reveal a segment of underserved nurses, and the findings resulted in a new value proposition that led to double-digit growth in less than six months. How did Coloplast achieve these results? To paraphrase hockey great Wayne Gretzky, Coloplast "skated to where the puck was going to be."

At the time, all other wound care companies had built their value propositions around some variation of "we help wounds heal faster." Coloplast realized that talking about speed of healing was akin to skating to where the puck had been. Sure, at some point in the past, wound care nurses had been underserved along that dimension and that value proposition had resonated with them. But those days were long gone.

When we conducted **Outcome-Based Segmentation** for Coloplast, we found a segment of wound care nurses whose top unmet needs had nothing to do with speed of healing. Instead, 10 of their top 15 unmet needs—their desired outcomes—related to "making sure the wound doesn't get worse." It turns out that in many wound treatment situations, the patient unwittingly makes the wound worse, and avoiding those complications was a challenge for nurses.

Coloplast realized that "preventing complications" was where the puck was going to be.

Coloplast went to market with its new wound care value proposition: "We prevent complications." Without changing its products or its pricing—simply by focusing its messaging and sales efforts on nurses' unmet outcomes—Coloplast achieved double-digit growth.

This is not an isolated incident. Our first success repositioning an existing product line was with Cordis Corporation back in 1992. Cordis experienced a 3-point increase in market share by aligning the strengths of its products with the unmet needs of the interventional cardiologist. In 2014, Arm & Hammer's Animal Nutrition division realigned its value proposition and achieved a 30%-plus increase in year-to-year revenue.

What is the secret to a winning value proposition?

The unmet needs of today represent the winning value propositions of the future. Knowing which needs are unmet—which desired outcomes are underserved—enables a company to secure a unique and valued competitive position. This is the essence of strategy, and it is best tackled through the effective use of Jobs Theory. To secure a winning value proposition, a company must (1) know where in the job the customer is underserved, (2) secure the value proposition that communicates to customers that their needs can be satisfied, and (3) do everything in its power to satisfy the targeted unmet needs better than its competitors.

The best way to figure out where the customer is underserved is through the application of **Outcome-Based Segmentation**. It was designed for this purpose. To create a winning value proposition, a company must know why a segment of customers is underserved, along which dimensions they are underserved, and to what degree. Once a company knows those three things, it can define a value proposition in a way that communicates its intent and ability to address all the unmet needs.

Once the value proposition is defined, the company must fulfill its promise. First, it must point out to customers ways in which its product or service already addresses the unmet needs it has discovered. Next, it must accelerate development of product and service features in the pipeline that further address the targeted unmet needs. Then it must create or invent new features that address any remaining unmet needs that are within the sphere of its value proposition. Coloplast worked over a period of years to address all the unmet needs associated with preventing complications.

A value proposition that is tied to unmet needs aligns company employees around a common vision and is integral to a company's long-term success.

VI. CONDUCT THE COMPETITIVE ANALYSIS

Why do you conduct competitive analysis? Is it merely to see which features of competitors' products are technically superior? Or is the goal to gain the insight that is needed to create products and services that get a job done better and/or more cheaply than competing solutions? We argue that the latter should be the goal. Therefore, comparing feature sets—"speeds and feeds"—of competing products is a waste of time. It's an outdated approach that provides irrelevant information.

We conduct competitive analysis by having customers quantitatively evaluate competing offerings against a complete set of desired outcome statements. That process reveals precisely which offerings get the job done better and which get it done worse. These customer insights help along two fronts: (1) they pinpoint precisely which desired outcomes to address to offset the strengths of competing offerings, and (2) they reveal what underserved desired outcomes exist in the market as a whole, thus offering a path for leapfrogging all competitors and establishing a unique and valued competitive position.

The same survey that is fielded to gather the data needed to perform the **Outcome-Based Segmentation** analysis is used to gather the information needed for this type of competitive analysis. In the survey we determine the importance of each desired outcome and the level of satisfaction users have with the leading products (the competitive product set).

Once this work is completed, an evaluation of competing products can begin. This can best be understood through the example of Bosch's ODI-based competitive analysis of the highly competitive North American circular-saw market.

DESIRED OUTCOME STATEMENT	IMP	SAT	OPP	DeWalt SAT	Makita SAT
Minimize the likelihood that debris flies up in the air when guiding the blade along the cut line, e.g., into the users face, eyes, etc.	8.9	3.2	14.5	3.1	3.3
Minimize the likelihood of inadvertently moving off the cut line/path when the cut path/line gets covered with dust	8.7	3.8	13.5	4.2	3.4
Minimize the time it takes to set the angle of the blade, e.g., make a bevel adjustment, etc.	8.6	4.1	13.0	5.0	3.6
Minimize the likelihood of snagging the cord on the material when making a long cut	8.2	3.7	12.7	3.8	3.6
Minimize the time it takes to place a saw back in service when the power cord is cut	7.0	2.5	11.5	2.5	2.5
Minimize the likelihood that the cut goes of track when finishing the cut	7.8	4.2	11.4	3.6	4.8
Minimize the time it takes to secure the saw from falling when it is not in use, e.g., from a ladder, rafter, etc.	6.7	2.7	10.7	3.0	2.6
Minimize the likelihood of dropping the saw when lowering it from a ladder/roof	7.8	5.1	10.5	5.0	4.8

First, we defined the customer and the Job-to-be-Done: tradesmen who are trying to "cut wood in a straight line." Then we captured 75 desired-outcome statements through customer interviews. Next, we surveyed 270 users of circular saws, including users of the two best-selling brands, DeWalt and Makita. We asked the users of those brands to rate the importance of each of the 75 outcomes and their level of satisfaction with the circular saw they used.

The table shows the results of that survey for eight of the outcome statements. It lists the outcome statement, the average importance of the outcome, the average satisfaction with the outcome, the opportunity score calculation, and the satisfaction scores of DeWalt and Makita circular-saw users.

With this type of quantitative data on each of the 75 outcome statements, Bosch was able to draw some solid conclusions:

- Bosch could determine which of the 75 desired outcomes were "table stakes," which are desired outcomes that were very important and very satisfied, but could not be ignored by a new Bosch entrant into the market.
- Bosch could see which outcomes were better satisfied by DeWalt and which were better satisfied by Makita. This not only revealed the strengths and weaknesses of each competitor, but enabled Bosch to

determine the technical reasons for their success, thus setting the direction for ideation.

- Because 14 of the 75 outcomes had an opportunity score greater than 10, Bosch could safely conclude that these 14 outcomes were underserved outcomes (unmet needs). Eight of these 14 outcomes are shown in the table above.

- Bosch knew that satisfying the 14 unmet outcomes significantly better than DeWalt and Makita would enable Bosch to occupy a unique and valued competitive position: it would be satisfying unmet needs that no other competitor had been able to satisfy. This is the essence of strategy and the reason for competitive analysis.

- Bosch could see whether and where DeWalt or Makita had strengths that were adding cost but not value, as represented by outcomes with strong satisfaction values, but low importance scores. With this insight, Bosch was able to avoid adding features that were unnecessary and costly.

ODI-based competitive analysis reveals customer insights that are not ordinarily available to an organization. Knowing how customers measure value and how competing offerings stack up enables an organization to create products and services that get the job done better and/or more cheaply, which is the ultimate goal of any innovation process.

VII. FORMULATE THE INNOVATION STRATEGY

Is there a way to choose an innovation strategy that relies on something other than gut feelings and hunches? The answer is yes: there is a highly reliable way to pick a winning innovation strategy. An innovation strategy, as we define it, is a plan that details which outcome-based segments and which underserved outcomes a company is going to target and how it is going to target them (either with existing offerings, improved products and services, or altogether new offerings). The innovation strategy also outlines the order in which the segments will be targeted and provides a timeline for implementation.

It's easiest to understand the process when you see it in action. Consider the work we did with the Bosch circular-saw product team. One segment we discovered through **Outcome-Based Segmentation** was comprised of tradesmen that mostly cut 2x4s. Customers in that segment were overserved because they were getting more benefits than they needed or wanted from the saws they were using. They made short cuts where precision did not matter and all their needs were satisfied. On the other extreme, we found a underserved segment of tradesmen who routinely made long, finish cuts that required precision, and who often had to make angle cuts that required them to adjust the blade height and angle. That segment had 14 unsatisfied outcomes.

With knowledge of these segments, we were able to formulate the innovation strategy. Success in any market comes by helping customers get a job done better and/or more cheaply, and Bosch had a number of options to consider. One option was to target the overserved segment with a circular saw that got the job done more cheaply (a disruptive strategy). While a viable option, it did not align with Bosch's desire to create a premium-brand circular saw for the North American market. Another option was to introduce new laser-based technology to the market. While this sounded exciting, that technology would have had little impact on getting the job done better and would have added to the cost, a sure recipe for failure.

The option that Bosch pursued was to stick with existing technology and to add features to the platform that would address the 14 underserved outcomes in the one underserved segment, yet cost less than competing solutions (a dominant strategy). **This was their innovation strategy.** They knew precisely what segment and unmet outcomes to target and what technology platform to use to achieve their goals. Bosch engineers addressed the unmet needs with the CS20 circular saw, which was the company's best-selling circular saw in North America for over 10 years.

When building an effective innovation strategy there is no room for hunches or guesswork: the qualitative, quantitative, and analytical methods that comprise our ODI process provide the insights needed to formulate a robust and reliable innovation strategy.

VIII. TARGET HIDDEN GROWTH OPPORTUNITIES

Deciding which unmet desired outcomes to target for growth is the essence of strategy and the most important decision a company will make. Everything a company does is tied to this decision.

To make this decision, we again rely on the statistically valid quantitative data we gathered to conduct the **Outcome-Based Segmentation** analysis. One quantitative study usually provides us with all the data we need to effectively execute the entire ODI process.

Once the outcome-based segments are discovered and segments are targeted for pursuit, we are ready to determine which unmet needs should be targeted in each segment to (i) help the customer get the job done better, and (ii) help the customer get the job done more cheaply.

To prioritize the opportunities, we employ the **"opportunity algorithm."** This algorithm enables us to determine which outcomes are (i) important to customers, and (ii) not satisfactorily achieved with the solution(s) they are currently using to get the job done.

THE OPPORTUNITY ALGORITHM

The mathematical formula we use is as follows:

Opportunity score = outcome importance + (outcome importance − outcome satisfaction)

This formula calculates the opportunity score for each desired outcome statement, thus revealing those that represent the best opportunities for growth. For example, if 200 out of 270 circular saw users (74% or 7.4 on our scale) rate the outcome "minimize the likelihood that the cut goes off track" a 4 or a 5 for importance (on a scale of 1–5, with 5 representing highest importance), and only 75 of the 270 users (28% or 2.8 on our scale) rate the satisfaction of the outcome a 4 or a 5 (on a scale of 1–5, with 5 representing greatest satisfaction), then that outcome has an opportunity score of $(7.4) + (7.4 - 2.8) = 12.0$. In our experience, an opportunity score of 10 or greater indicates that the outcome is underserved.

THE OPPORTUNITY LANDSCAPE

The opportunity landscape shows visually which outcomes are under-and overserved. As shown in the figure, there are three main sections: (1) the underserved section (on the right), which includes all outcomes with an opportunity score of 10 or greater, (2) the appropriately served section (in the middle), and (3) the overserved section (on the left), in which outcomes' satisfaction exceeds their importance.

All the outcomes included in the quantitative survey are plotted on this landscape, revealing with a high degree of precision where the targeted segment is under-and overserved.

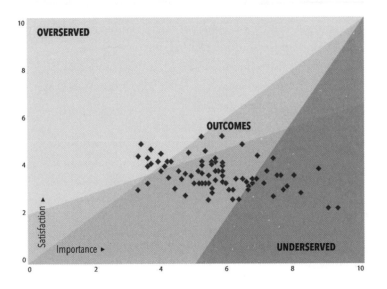

This approach clearly points out which outcomes to target for growth. The upper right section of the landscape points out the "table stakes," which are important outcomes that existing products satisfy and that new products must also satisfy to win in the marketplace. The overserved outcomes in the left-most area become targets for cost reduction. If existing products include costly features that address these overserved outcomes, replacing them with lower-cost features can help customers get the job done more cheaply.

The outcomes in the lower part of the shaded area on the right are the most underserved. Addressing those outcomes will enable the customer to get the job done better.

Ask yourself what the chances are of developing a product or service that addresses underserved outcomes if the development team doesn't know what those underserved outcomes—unmet needs—are. You will rightly conclude that the chances are extremely low.

But what if the development team knows precisely what those underserved outcomes are? The chances for success go up dramatically. This is the power of **Outcome-Driven Innovation.**

The opportunity algorithm and the opportunity landscape are invaluable tools when trying to figure out which outcomes to target for growth.

IX. FORMULATE THE MARKET STRATEGY

The **Outcome-Driven Innovation** process includes qualitative research methods that are used to discover the customer's Job-to-be-Done and their desired outcomes. It also includes quantitative research methods that are used to discover outcome-based segments of opportunity and to identify which desired outcomes in each segment are underserved—these are needs that are unmet. With this information in hand, a company has the customer-centric, data-driven inputs it needs to formulate a market strategy.

An effective market strategy should align the strengths of a company's product offerings with the customer's unmet needs. This is best accomplished through the marketing activities shown in the figure below. We recommend the following steps:

(1) Decide which offerings to target at each outcome-based segment.
(2) Communicate the strengths of those offerings to customers in the target segment.
(3) Include an outcome-based value proposition in communications.
(4) Build a digital marketing strategy around unmet outcomes.
(5) Assign leads to ODI-based segments.
(6) Arm the sales team with effective sales tools.

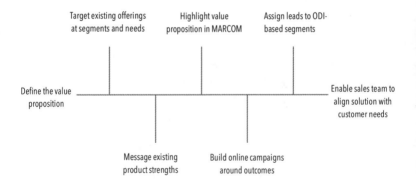

Let's look at how each element of the market strategy is enhanced when it is informed by outcome-based market research.

Decide which offerings to target at each outcome-based segment

The first step in defining the market strategy is to determine which current product offerings to target at each of the outcome-based segments that have been discovered. This should be decided based on "fit": choose the offerings that best satisfy the unmet outcomes of customers in each outcome-based segment. For example, we once helped a manufacturer of industrial pumps discover a segment of customers that were underserved because they frequently encountered conditions that led to cavitation (the formation of air bubbles). The company had a number of products that addressed this problem well, but it had never targeted those products at the underserved segment with the right messaging. Knowing to target those offerings at that segment was the first step to success.

Communicate the strengths of those offerings to customers in the target segment

In one of Strategyn's first engagements, we helped Cordis discover that one of its existing products satisfied a number of outcomes that were not well satisfied by top competing offerings. The "un-messaged strengths" of this product were subsequently communicated to customers. The result was a significant increase in market share: from 1.5% to 5% over the next six months. Knowing that a product has features that are a competitive strength in a segment of the market is an important insight when it comes to aligning a product portfolio with customer needs.

Include an outcome-based value proposition in communications

Using ODI, Coloplast's wound care division discovered a segment of wound care nurses that had 15 underserved outcomes, 10 of which were associated with making sure a wound did not get worse. While Coloplast's competitors focused on how their products helped wounds heal faster, Coloplast decided to go with an outcome-based value proposition. It promoted the fact that its products would "prevent complications" and highlighted the product features that addressed the associated outcomes. With this new value proposition, the company achieved double-digit growth in less than six months.

Build a digital marketing strategy around unmet outcomes

When potential customers use Google to find and evaluate product alternatives, they rarely start by entering the product name and model because they have yet to discover it. Rather, they enter keywords or phrases that are associated with the "Job-to-be-Done," such as a job step or a specific desired outcome they are trying to achieve. With ODI-based research, these keywords and phrases are known to the company, which can use them as the foundation for online campaigns, dramatically improving buyer awareness of its product. Any time a potential customer uses Google to find out how to address an unmet outcome they will see the company's ad and find its product. A similar strategy can be used to improve SEO results for those same keywords.

Assign leads to ODI-based segments

Many companies process all leads in the same way even though customers have different unmet outcomes. However, using a short 5–10 question survey (on a website or lead-generation tool), a company can accurately determine which outcome-based segment a specific prospect belongs to. With this insight, the prospect can be guided toward the solution that will best address their underserved outcomes.

Arm the sales team with effective sales tools

Lastly, the sales team can be taught how to identify what outcome-based segment a customer or prospect belongs to and guide the conversation accordingly. Approaching a customer with the right value proposition and a clear understanding of their situation and unmet needs goes a long way to building credibility. In 2014, Arm & Hammer's Animal Nutrition Division used ODI to align its offerings, messaging, and sales efforts around certain underserved segments and outcomes it had discovered. The result was impressive: the Animal Nutrition Division achieved 30% year-to-year revenue growth from 2013 to 2014 without changing its product or pricing—a clear demonstration of the power of aligning marketing and sales efforts around the customer's Job-to-be-Done.

X. FORMULATE THE PRODUCT STRATEGY

An effective product portfolio strategy will guide a company in (i) improving its products to better serve the unmet needs of customers in each targeted outcome-based segment, and (ii) will offer a solution that eventually gets the entire job done on a single platform.

Once the underserved outcome-based segments are uncovered and prioritized, the company can take the seven courses of action shown in the figure below for each segment:

(1) Borrow features from other company offerings.
(2) Accelerate offerings in the pipeline and R&D.
(3) Partner with or license from other firms.
(4) Acquire another firm to fill a gap.
(5) Devise a new feature set.
(6) Devise new subsystems and/or ancillary services.
(7) Conceptualize the ultimate solution.

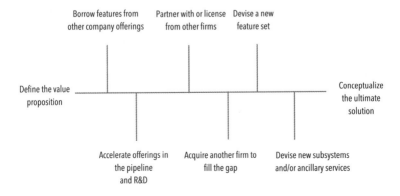

Let's look at how each activity is enhanced when it is informed by outcome-based market research.

Borrow features from other company offerings

Why reinvent the wheel? Innovation does not necessarily require invention. Innovation is the ability to use technology (existing or new) to address an unmet customer need. Knowing exactly what outcomes are underserved in a target segment, a company can analyze its product portfolio to see if any of its current products or services possesses a feature that addresses one or more of those outcomes. This can save significant development time and effort.

When we helped Microsoft discover opportunities to improve its software assurance offering, it turned out that many of those opportunities could be addressed with tools the company used internally to get the job done. Instead of starting from scratch, the assurance teams were able to package internal products for commercial use.

A catalog of product features and the desired outcomes they address could be a valuable asset for any company, but especially for big company with hundreds or even thousands of offerings. Such a tool makes it possible for product teams across the company to leverage what the company has already invented.

Accelerate offerings in the pipeline and R&D

When we helped Cordis discover opportunities in the angioplasty balloon market, one underserved outcome rose to the top of the list: "minimize the likelihood of restenosis"—that is, the recurrence of the blockage. Upon receiving this insight, my contacts at the company told me that the R&D team was working on a device, called a stent, which had the potential to address this unmet outcome. Recognizing the size of the opportunity and the importance of being first to market, the R&D team put additional resources on the project and was the first to market with a product that generated $1 billion dollars in revenue over the next few years.

The stent had already been in the works, but it was just one of about 40 initiatives in total. It was only when the company gathered and prioritized its customers' underserved desired outcomes that it realized that the stent deserved more funds and attention. Other initiatives were less lucky: those that did not speak to customers' needs were defunded altogether.

Leveraging efforts that are all ready under way can save time and effort when creating products and services that will get the job done better.

Partner with or license from other firms

We have often worked with hardware manufacturers that discover many of the underserved outcomes remaining in the market cannot be addressed with a hardware solution: a software or service offering is required. At that point, it makes sense to partner with or license from a firm that has expertise in that area.

Knowing precisely what needs are underserved makes choosing a partner easier. For example, we worked with an automobile manufacturer that discovered it did not have the capabilities it needed to address the underserved outcomes in a market of interest. With the list of prioritized underserved outcomes in hand, we evaluated over 100 possible partners. The goal was to look at the potential partners and determine how well they could address each of the underserved outcomes. Through this analysis, we found the three firms that held the most promise. The company interviewed management from the three firms and eventually picked an effective partner.

A prioritized list of underserved outcomes makes the perfect scorecard against which to evaluate firms that will help you get more of a job done and/or get the job done better.

Acquire another firm to fill a gap

Arm & Hammer's Animal Nutrition Group acquired a business, Vi-COR, that provided it with a complimentary product to use in its dairy business. The framework they used to help justify the acquisition was grounded in ODI-based research: the group was able to demonstrate that its current offering failed to get the entire job done and showed that Vi-

COR's products were going to help address some high-priority underserved outcomes.

Vi-COR also provided a service component that helped address other top opportunities identified in dairies. Company management determined that Vi-COR was operating in a very important niche, providing a very important solution to dairy producers. Without the ODI prioritized list of underserved outcomes, the company might have overlooked this important potential acquisition.

Devise a new feature set
Knowing what features to add to a product to help customers get more of the job done and/or get the job done better is the key to success in product innovation. Adding the right features is dependent on knowing what needs are underserved. Knowing, for example, which 15 of the customer's 100 desired outcomes are underserved lets a company focus its efforts on those 15, thereby ending wasted effort and increasing the chances of success to a dramatic 86 percent.

Companies do not lack ideas. They often have thousands of ideas. What they need is insight into the customer's underserved outcomes. This is what the ODI process provides. Once everybody in the organization knows precisely what the customer's unmet outcomes are, all company resources can be aligned to address them—

resulting in the systematic and predictable creation of customer value.

Devise new subsystems and/or ancillary services

Hardware and technology-based companies often stunt their growth potential because they resist adding a necessary service component. When the entire Job-to-be-Done is defined and the underserved outcomes are revealed, however, a company comes face to face with the fact that the only way to satisfy the remaining underserved outcomes is by adding an ancillary service offering. With a list of underserved outcomes in hand, a company can define exactly what value the service offering must deliver.

Advanced Medical Optics followed this approach when it added a service offering to complement its sale of lenses, insertion systems, laser vision correction systems, and other devices for cataract and refractive surgical procedures. Offering this service had immediate positive results on its Net Promoter score, the perception of its overall business practices, and its customer loyalty index. Two years later, AMO was awarded the prestigious Omega Management NorthFace Award, which recognizes world-class customer satisfaction.

Conceptualize the ultimate solution

A company's ultimate goal should be to provide an offering that gets the entire job done on a single platform. Such a platform often requires hardware, software, and service subsystems or components. Conceptualizing this ultimate solution provides a company with a long-term vision of where it needs to go and what will be necessary to secure or maintain a market leadership position.

With the ultimate solution in mind, a company is in a position to make the decisions that will allow it to stay on track, stay focused, and not let a competitor own the ultimate platform-level solution.

For example, the ultimate solution we presented to an agricultural company we were working with required skills and capabilities that went far beyond the company's capabilities at that time. As the years went by, the company watched a competitor make the acquisitions that were required to create, build, and own this platform-level solution. This got management's attention. With no time to waste and clarity in where the market was heading, the company worked to make its own acquisitions so it could remain relevant in the market.

Taking the seven steps outline above, a company can systematically create solutions that will get a job done better and/or more cheaply. Defining the actions it will take is the essence of an effective product strategy.

5.
CASE STUDIES

MICROSOFT

Discovering hidden growth opportunities

Microsoft was under pressure to build additional value into its Software Assurance offering. In exchange for a flat fee, corporate customers received operating system upgrade rights if they signed a multiyear contract.

However, there was mounting evidence that the offering was not providing the right mix of benefits to customers at a time when IT budgets were facing increased scrutiny. Microsoft was aware that some key customers were questioning the value of the offering. Even more telling, renewals of Software Assurance agreements were declining, putting a significant amount of potential revenue at risk. "We were a business facing a potential crisis," recalls Dave Wascha, a Microsoft director.

Traditionally, Microsoft had viewed the Software Assurance offering simply as a vehicle for the efficient purchase of software upgrades. The market was changing, however, and Microsoft realized that the Software Assurance offering needed to change with it. As one tech reporter observed, "There appears to be some disconnect between how Microsoft wants to sell its software and how businesses want to buy." Improvements were necessary to give customers additional reasons to purchase.

Software license management is not a trivial task for large corporations, and it typically involves multiple stakeholders. Microsoft focused on understanding the jobs of two particular decision makers—procurement managers and IT professionals. Procurement managers are responsible for understanding, selecting, and negotiating license agreements (the Job-to-be-Done). IT professionals work closely with procurement managers in assessing upgrade needs, evaluating agreements, implementing licensing renewals, and managing software licenses once purchased (their Job-to-be-Done).

Drawing on interviews with procurement managers, the ODI practitioner dissected the job of purchasing a license agreement, uncovering approximately 75 desired outcome statements. Customer interviews were also conducted with IT professionals, resulting in the discovery of well over 100 desired outcome statements related to their core functional Job-to-be-Done and related job statements.

Two ODI-based quantitative surveys were created and deployed. Approximately 100 procurement managers and 300 IT professionals prioritized their respective desired outcome statements for importance and level of satisfaction.

The results of the **Outcome-Based Segmentation** analysis revealed underserved segments of procurement managers and IT professionals. Dozens of underserved outcomes were revealed for each constituent. Wascha recalls that as they started to look at the job the customers were trying to get done, "we realized that we were only really engaging with the customer in one tiny piece of their job— the purchase of the software. But this was just part of a much bigger challenge that they faced. We were not engaging with them in many of these other areas that were very important to them and where they were very dissatisfied."

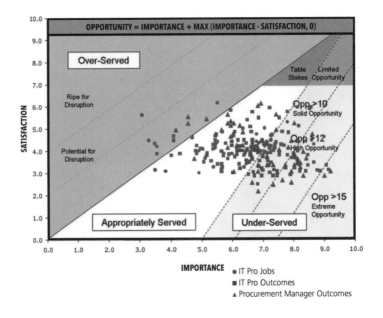

The opportunity landscape for purchasing and managing software licenses revealed a number of jobs and desired outcomes that were underserved. Many could be addressed by products already developed, but not previously integrated into the offering.

Based on this improved understanding of the job its customers were trying to accomplish, Microsoft adopted a lifecycle management view of the business, from the customer's perspective. Microsoft discovered opportunities related to software acquisition and deployment at the start of the lifecycle. In the middle of the lifecycle, there were opportunities in the areas of maintenance, training, patching, and security. Finally, at the end of the lifecycle, Microsoft identified opportunities to create value for customers during disposal of old PCs—an immense issue for many of its customers.

The innovation and the impact

One of Microsoft's most profound discoveries was that the company had already developed many solutions for internal use that would help customers achieve their desired outcomes and get jobs done, given this broader lifecycle perspective.

However, those solutions had never been packaged together in a cohesive and compelling offering. Wascha notes, "The most amazing thing is that we really did not write that many new lines of code to meet customer needs. Rather, it was about looking at the job in its flowchart, looking at software assets that we already had, and then piecing them together as solutions to each part of the job.

For example, Microsoft discovered that customers were having trouble keeping track of the number of PC software licenses they owned—a necessary step in compliance. Microsoft already had a licensing server that could address this need, but the company had never considered including it as a part of the Software Assurance offering. Similarly, IT professionals were having difficulty anticipating potential software conflicts when they deployed a new operating system. Again, Microsoft already had a tool that could address this need, one that the company had been using internally. Microsoft decided to include a version of that tool in its Software Assurance offering.

Customers also wanted to reduce the time and cost involved in training employees to use the upgraded software. To address this, Microsoft implemented a training voucher program that gave employees access to certified Microsoft trainers. Once again, this was a program that Microsoft had already developed but had never been made a formal component of the Software Assurance offering.

Microsoft also uncovered an unmet need related to prevention of internal security violations. As in the other examples, Microsoft already had a successful product that it was able to make part of the Software Assurance package.

The product included rule templates that enabled companies to quickly set software and PC access restrictions for different groups of employees—a key element of internal security. And the list of enhancements to the Software Assurance offering could go on.

The benefits to Microsoft from adopting the ODI approach were dramatic and immediate. In the year Microsoft announced the changes to the Software Assurance offering, they beat their revenue goal by over 10 percent. This was even before the fully revised product was available. Customer satisfaction increased, and complaints about Software Assurance dropped.

In subsequent years, Microsoft was able to substantially grow the Software Assurance business and dramatically increase annual renewal rates. Microsoft discovered it was sitting on a growth business once value was measured from the customer's perspective. Wascha noted, "Salespeople loved the new product offering. They felt they had something of value to offer."

KROLL ONTRACK

Discovering hidden growth opportunities

Kroll Ontrack was faced with a strategic opportunity and a challenge. The opportunity lay in the potential market for an electronic document discovery solution for the legal industry.

The challenge? Creating an effective market strategy for a business still in its infancy.

"The term 'paperless office' was just coming into vogue," notes Andrea Johnson, Kroll Ontrack's vice president of marketing and communications. Lawyers were finding that many documents relevant to a legal proceeding were available only in electronic form. Competitors who had historically served the market were able to meet the paper discovery needs of lawyers but were ill equipped to manage the discovery of these electronic records.

In response to a client's request, Kroll Ontrack started a small business focused on electronic document discovery. It struggled at first to define a strategy based on customer needs. As Ben Allen, CEO of Kroll and former Kroll Ontrack president, explains, "We knew the potential for electronic discovery—all of the underlying foundational elements suggested that this would be an important industry opportunity. What we didn't know was how to understand what clients wanted to achieve in a way that could be translated into an efficient and effective strategy for growth. The electronic discovery market was so new that if you asked clients what features they wanted, they didn't know what you were talking about."

In order to define a market strategy for a product offering that was still in its infancy, Kroll Ontrack relied on Strategyn's ODI methodology. "After going home and reading 17 strategy books," Allen recalls, "what struck me about Strategyn's ODI thinking was the concept that outcomes wouldn't change over time. We were really at the stage where we were trying to figure out what lawyers were trying to accomplish, not what features they wanted."

Drawing on interviews with lawyers (the end users), the ODI practitioner uncovered approximately 100 desired outcome statements related to "finding information that supported/refuted their case" (the Job-to-be-Done). The outcome statements were rated for importance and satisfaction by a statistically valid sample of the population. **Outcome-Based Segmentation** and other analyses were performed.

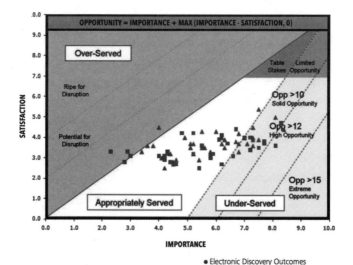

- Electronic Discovery Outcomes
- Information Management Outcomes

Using ODI, Kroll Ontrack gained a better understanding of the opportunities presented by electronic discovery, and it used this knowledge to develop an effective product strategy. Kroll Ontrack focused on the job of e-document discovery and the outcomes that members of the legal community desired, which led the company to develop groundbreaking new solutions.

For example, Kroll Ontrack rolled out a new product called Harvester and some related imaging tools that addressed the top two underserved electronic discovery outcomes: "Minimize the likelihood that relevant documents were excluded from capture" and "Minimize the likelihood that information is inadvertently altered or destroyed while the data is being captured." Because two other outcomes, "Minimize the likelihood of making coding errors" and "Minimize the time that it takes to obtain all information relating to a specific subject," were also important, Kroll Ontrack added a custom-coding feature to its online review tool.

The ODI-based research guided the pursuit of numerous other innovations as well. For example, Kroll acquired a clever search technology that employs clustering algorithms to enable a user to find documents associated with a keyword even if that keyword does not occur in the document. This was done to satisfy two of the outcome opportunities identified. In addition, Kroll Ontrack launched ESI

Consulting, which offers clients expert guidance in tackling the task of capturing all relevant documents. Lastly, it rolled out a new trial preparation tool that targeted litigation process outcomes.

Reflecting on the top opportunities that the ODI methodology revealed, Allen recalls, "There has been a ton of innovation at Kroll around these outcomes. These are the heart of it. We brought forward all elements that an electronic document has available and made them available to filter or search by. And we have continued to add features along the way." By adding innovative features to its electronic discovery platform every quarter to address additional underserved outcomes, it made it very difficult for competitors to catch them.

Kroll Ontrack's electronic discovery product employed a dominant strategy—it got the job done better and more cheaply than competing solutions. Prior to Kroll Ontrack, competitors had been attempting to address the challenges presented by electronic documents with modifications to the paper document discovery systems. In contrast, "Kroll Ontrack leapfrogged the competition with a revolutionary innovation," observes Johnson, "because it added capabilities based on the job that customers were trying to get done rather than seeking to improve the current solution platform."

A myopic definition of the market ultimately cost the leading competitors their discovery business. Allen concludes, "If these big, well-established companies had understood the outcomes that customers really valued, they could have dominated this business. I think they saw themselves as paper document processing companies, not discovery solutions providers. The leaders today—none of them were players in the old paper discovery business."

Kroll's market strategy has paid off. Kroll Ontrack grew is revenue in this market from $11 million in to over $200 million in about 6 years. For years, Kroll Ontrack was the industry leader in both market share and revenues. They received acclaim from industry experts and customers for quality and were named the top electronic data discovery system by readers of Law Technology News. They were also recognized by Law Firm Inc. as the most-used electronic discovery provider for seven years in a row.

ARM & HAMMER

Arm & Hammer's Animal Nutrition business (Church & Dwight) was determined to grow. Scott Druker, director of the business, chose to employ Strategyn and its Outcome-Driven Innovation methodology to formulate and drive its growth strategy. **A mere year after adopting Strategyn's "Jobs-to-be-Done" thinking, the business experienced over 30% revenue growth, far**

outpacing its competitors. Scott sat down with Tony Ulwick to talk about their journey.

Ulwick: Scott, how would you describe the problem that Church & Dwight was trying to solve?

Druker: We had gone through several product development efforts and launches in recent years that were disappointing despite the technical success of the products. The commercial response was lackluster. So, not wanting to repeat history and recognizing that innovation was an important aspect of our growth strategy, we asked ourselves, "Okay, how can we do things differently?" I was familiar with your work, and I thought it would be an interesting approach to take given the challenges we were facing with our animal nutrition products in the dairy market.

How would you describe Arm & Hammer Animal Nutrition's traditional approach to innovation?

We relied largely on discussions that we'd had with customers, with people in the industry that we worked in, the dairy industry in particular. We'd talk to nutritionists and to dairy producers, asking, "What are some of your biggest issues?" We mainly focused on the nutritionists, who are the people the dairy producer hires to help put together the ration to feed the cows. Our products go into those rations, so even though the dairy producers are buying the products, most of our efforts were focused on the nutritionists.

Would it be fair to say that before using ODI, part of the issue was not knowing which customer to target to obtain the needed insights?

We've always known the end customer is the dairy producer, and ultimately the dairy cow, but yeah, we were basically getting our innovation information from a consultant that was being hired by the dairy producer. So yeah, I think absolutely part of our issue was we weren't identifying the right people to speak to.

Why did you choose to go with Strategyn and ODI over other options?

Prior to joining Church & Dwight and taking lead of the Arm & Hammer nutrition business, I led a business that sold anti-microbial actives and formulated products, and I was responsible for developing markets and new products. I first came across the ODI concept while reading The Innovator's Solution, by Clayton Christensen. That book makes reference to your work and the concept of Jobs-to-be-Done, and that led me to read your book, What Customers Want. It was natural for me to decide that if I was going to do something to improve innovation, I might as well go to the people who wrote the book on it.

We're happy that you did. Let's talk about the results. What surprising insights came out of the Strategyn/ODI research?

The research helped on many fronts. First, it helped clarify in our minds that the customer is the dairy producer, not the nutritionist. Next, understanding that the "job" they were trying to get done had little to do with nutrition and was focused squarely on optimizing herd productivity. Then it was certainly eye opening to see how many desired outcomes the dairy producer is trying to satisfy in a given day, in a given month, in a given year. I think we identified over 165 different desired outcomes (well-constructed need statements). We homed in on optimizing dairy herd productivity, and when we started prioritizing the outcomes through quantitative research, the most surprising thing was how many opportunities there were, and how few of those opportunities were directly related to nutritional ingredients for the dairy producer. Our whole business is focused on supplying nutritional ingredients and supplements, so that was probably the most surprising thing.

Scott, how would you describe the market strategy that Strategyn recommended based on the customer insights?

Clearly the market strategy started with our collective recognition of whom we needed to target for value creation. Even though we don't sell directly to the dairy producer, we need to make sure that we keep our eye on the dairy producer and the job they are trying to get done. We have relationships with various other components in the supply chain, but at the end of the day, we need to create value for the dairy producer.

The second major focus was changing our messaging and how we speak about things—moving away from talking about product benefits and features and toward talking about outcomes, and linking our products to the outcomes they satisfied. The third focus was taking a look at the job map, which had 15 steps in it, and saying, "Let's take a step back and look at where we can position ourselves in the marketplace that impacts the majority of these steps."

The other part of the market strategy is segmentation: recognizing that the normal demographic methods for segmenting customers, while helpful for sales resource prioritization, are not helpful for opportunity identification, and hence solution identification. One of the things I go back to, one of the surprising things that came out of the research, was that a large dairy or mega dairy can share many of the same unmet needs and outcomes as a small dairy. And geography wasn't necessarily the determinant either: ultimately there were some key outcomes that decided what kind of segmentation there was. Thinking about that—the segments and how we position the business—has become an important part of our marketing strategy.

How did the Outcome-Based Segmentation solution impact your market strategy?

Outcome-Based Segmentation gave us a more realistic way to look at the market. Over time we had confused sales prioritization with real customer market segmentation. At the end of the day, we only have a certain number of salespeople, so we tend to want to call on the larger dairies, because if you get one of them, they have a measurable impact on your business. We just assumed that all those large dairies share certain needs, and that small dairies have completely different needs. The data showed that was not the case, so that absolutely was surprising.

What other market strategy recommendations provided your team with immediate value?

One of the key recommendations that we initially focused on was to go after the low-hanging fruit, to find out if and where our existing products addressed some of the most underserved outcomes that were identified. We basically got into a room, listed 165 of the outcomes on the wall, color coded the segmentation, and identified the 10 or 11 outcomes that all segments shared and identified as high priorities. We literally went through each one of our products and tried to see which outcomes those products could potentially help address.

We then focused a lot on the redesign of our whole messaging. We took all our product literature and our website and redesigned and focused them on outcomes. Our whole marketing talk and speak turned to outcome based, and that is very prevalent now in our whole business. People talk about outcomes. Now you hear salespeople saying, "We need to position this in terms of an outcome a person is trying to satisfy." So that is rewarding, to hear people starting to think that way. I think some of the basic elements of the recommendations we followed pretty quickly.

There were several recommendations made around becoming a total solution provider to the dairy. We probably have been a little slower to respond on that, but it's not ignored; it's probably something I am spending more time on now, thinking about.

Was there a reason the organization was ready for change?

Yes. We had a product—a protective license product—that we had developed and launched. We spent seven years developing it based on hearing in the market that there was a need for it. I would argue and defend it as the best in the market, and we launched it to much fanfare. Then it kind of just did a ho-hum. So that example was fresh in our teams' minds, and we could say, "What went wrong here?" It's not the product development, and certainly not our marketing. It's certainly not our company's reputation, and it's not our overall knowledge of who to call on, or our ability to access any of the particular decision makers. It's just that we didn't ask the right people the right questions. That was probably one of the easiest ways to start convincing people: we had just had a fresh example of a product innovation that was just lackluster.

Of all the actions taken to date, which had the most impact on revenue?

Clearly, changing our messaging helped us differentiate our products versus competitors'. Whenever you pick up a trade journal in our industry, you see a cow in an ad and virtually the same story: "We can help improve milk production, protein production, fat production, dry matter intake." It doesn't matter which ad you are looking at; it is virtually the same thing. So what we have been able to do is say, that's not really what the people are focused on. It's actually surprising when you think about it. Of the 165 outcomes that the dairy producer mentioned, not one of them identified any of those key points that you see in almost every one of the ads. So we didn't necessarily have to go change our pricing or products or redesign or reformulate the products. The biggest impact was changing the messaging so people understood, "Oh that's what that product can help me get done."

Can you describe how the market strategy implementation rolled out?

By the end of 2013 we got all the results, and we spent the end of 2013 really going through the first stage of looking at our products, digesting the information, and asking ourselves, "Okay, how do we act on this data?" Second, we tried to understand how our products could address some of the underserved outcomes, and we started thinking about the segments and how we should change some of our sales conversations, based on what segments a customer might fall into. By the time 2014 rolled around, we had really started the wholesale change to be forward facing to the market—changing our positioning and our Web design and promotional literature. By the first quarter of 2014 and certainly by the second quarter of 2014, we were full on into repositioning how we go into the marketplace.

How long did it take for you to start seeing results?

I would say we started to see results almost immediately. You start seeing the results in terms of the conversations you are having, and then you start seeing incorporation of products. We had a phenomenal 2014. Off the charts. The dairy economy helped—it was a factor in it. I think our execution, our messaging, and our positioning all contributed to an outstanding year.

Can you share how the ODI-based market strategy impacted your revenue growth?

I'll say we grew revenue greater than 30% and the ODI process played a significant role in that growth. Every one of our products had double-digit growth.

In addition, in January 2015, we made an acquisition of a business, Vi-COR, that got us into more species than just dairy. It brought a very nice complimentary product for us to use in dairy, but it also got us into the poultry and swine markets, which is exciting for the growth of our business. When we made this acquisition, the template I used to explain to our executive team why it made sense was generated from the ODI work. I was able to show them that here is a job map, and here are outcomes the dairy producer is trying to satisfy, and here is why Vi-COR's products are going to help us with some of these key outcomes. Vi-COR also brings in a service component that helps address some areas that we identified as some of the top opportunities in dairies. I found that this small business was operating in a very important niche, providing a very important solution to dairy producers. I used the work from ODI to screen for acquisitions, and that work assisted in the acquisition.

How did these successes impact the organization and you personally?

Probably the biggest personal gratification I have is looking at my team and seeing that they are embracing the methodology. I think it helped them think more broadly about who we are as a business and what we do, and what opportunities are out there.

How would you describe your experience working with Strategyn?

It was terrific. I believe the agriculture nutrition industry was a little bit outside of where Strategyn normally works. All the same, you guys are great, professional, intelligent, right on time. Great communications—it was definitely really enjoyable to work with the group. And I speak for my whole team.

That is always good to hear. Thank you. And just as a final question, is there anything else you would like us to share with the readers of this case study?

That no one else in agriculture should try this! But more seriously, the thing that I would share is, once you get involved and you start to think about a market through this lens, the notion of defining your customer as a job executor, and then asking customers what job they are trying to get done instead of asking them what solutions they want is such a basic, simple, and obvious way to approach product development. It's remarkable that companies just don't do it more often. But I do understand why. It's not trivial to do. I've come to appreciate that it's not an easy exercise, but once you have gone through it, it's so obvious – and powerful. It is obviously the right way to approach marketing and innovation.

BOSCH

Discovering hidden growth opportunities

When the Robert Bosch Tool Company decided to enter the North American professional circular saw market, many challenges stood in the way of their success. Randall Coe, director of product development, noted that management had four key objectives in mind: "We wanted to (1) enter the market with a saw that reflected the high-quality image carried by the Bosch name, (2) compete effectively and outperform the products produced by DeWalt and other competitors in the U.S. market, (3) ensure our product would be carried by the big-box retailers, e.g., Home Depot and Lowe's, and (4) price the resulting product at a competitive industry price point while yielding the desired profit margin."

There had not been much innovation in the circular saw market for many years, and it was perceived as both mature and commodity-like, so Bosch knew that success would depend on the company's ability to uncover and inexpensively address market opportunities that others had missed.

To identify opportunities for product innovation, the Bosch team targeted professional tradesmen (the job executors) who were responsible for cutting wood in a straight line (the Job-to-be-Done). They targeted roofers, framers, contractors, finish carpenters, plumbers and electricians.

Through interviews with the professional tradesmen, the ODI practitioner dissected the Job-to-be-Done into its component parts through the use of a job map and worked to capture a complete set of approximately 85 desired outcome statements.

Next, ODI-based quantitative research methods were employed. Through a controlled online survey, approximately 270 professional tradesmen rated each desired outcome statement for (i) its level of importance, and (ii) the degree to which it was satisfied, given the circular saws they were currently using. This data was used to run a variety of data analyses (Outcome-Based Segmentation, competitive analysis, etc.).

Not surprisingly, the results showed that in the market on average (when looking at all 270 responses combined), there were no unmet needs. This meant that to discover unmet needs, **Outcome-Based Segmentation** practices were required. Strategyn's Outcome-Based Segmentation methods revealed four segments of opportunity, one of which made a perfect target for Bosch. This hidden segment of opportunity, which was comprised of primarily finish and advanced carpenters, represented over 30 percent of all users. They were underserved because they made more finish and angle cuts and had to make frequent blade angle and blade height adjustments. The segmentation analysis and opportunity landscape for this segment clearly revealed that 14 of the customer's approximately 85 desired outcomes were unmet with this segment of users.

Knowing where to focus its efforts was the key to Bosch's success, as it dramatically simplified idea generation.

The innovation and the impact

The team went through the list of 14 opportunities, systematically generating ideas that would better satisfy each underserved outcome. Coe reports, "We started by focusing on the underserved outcomes related to the cord and devised the Direct Connect™ cord system concept. This innovation, which connects the extension cord directly to the saw, reduces the chances that users will cut the cord or catch the plug on the material being cut when making a long cut while maintaining their ability to lower the tool from a ladder to the ground using the cord. This system also reduces repair costs and down time because if the cord gets cut, the user can simply grab another extension cord and continue working. Satisfying all these outcomes at the same time is what made this a true innovation."

"Next," Coe says, "we focused on line-of-sight issues and devised a way in which the user can confirm that the cut is on track when starting the cut, while making the cut, and when approaching the end of the board. Designing a cutout in the table helped to better satisfy all of these underserved outcomes." The team went on to address the remaining unmet outcomes, in all cases devising low-cost features that would dramatically improve customer satisfaction.

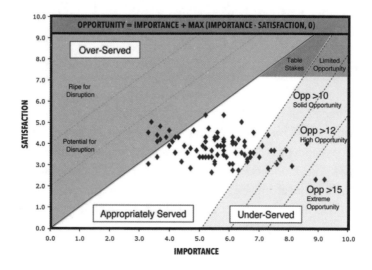

Bosch successfully addressed the 14 underserved outcomes in the newly discovered segment with a new product—the CS20 circular saw—that successfully addressed each of them. Remarkably, Bosch accomplished this without increasing product cost—a prime management objective. This was largely due to the fact that the highly regarded Direct Connect™ system significantly cut product cost while adding customer value.

Most successful new products and services improve customers' satisfaction in areas of unmet needs by less than 10 percent, but concept testing revealed that the CS20 circular saw was projected to increase the level of customer satisfaction by approximately 38 percent (with total satisfaction levels rising from 63 to 87 percent).

Before the saw was released, the Bosch team used these findings to help gain the support of two key distributors: Lowe's and Home Depot. Given limited shelf space and a competitive market, Bosch had to convince them that the CS20 circular saw uniquely addressed a number of unmet customer needs and did so at a competitive price. The data made a convincing case, and Lowe's and Home Depot requested that Bosch delay the release of the product by two months so that enough saws could be manufactured to meet the anticipated demand.

Bosch successfully entered the North American market with what quickly became one of the top-selling and top-rated circular saws. Bosch's innovations, which addressed cord and line-of-sight issues, resulted in a highly successful product launch and dramatic improvements in customer satisfaction. Improvements in handling, adjustments, and other functions only added to the new value created.

Upon its introduction, the CS20 circular saw won accolades from Popular Science, being voted one of the top 100 innovative products of the year.

ABBOTT MEDICAL OPTICS

Discovering hidden growth opportunities

Abbott Medical Optics, or AMO (formerly Advanced Medical Optics), is a leading provider of lenses, insertion systems, laser vision correction systems, and other devices for cataract and refractive surgical procedures.

Historically a technology-based company, AMO recognized the need to improve its approach to service innovation in an effort to attract and retain customers through secondary service offerings. Angelo Rago, AMO's senior vice president of global customer services, noted that a cycle of incremental service improvements had resulted in "me too" service delivery mechanisms and support services— services that looked just like AMO's competitors' offerings. Worse, Rago and his team recognized that sales were being lost to competitors due to poor customer service.

To identify opportunities for service innovation, AMO targeted the materials managers (the job executors) who were responsible for replenishing ophthalmic lenses for cataract implant surgeries (the Job-to-be-Done). They targeted medical facilities in which cataract surgeries were performed.

Through interviews with materials managers, the ODI practitioner dissected the Job-to-be-Done into its component parts through the use of a job map and worked to capture a complete set of approximately 100 desired outcome statements. By studying the job map, AMO discovered that a traditional distinction between front-office and back-office responsibilities for materials management was artificial.

Next, ODI-based quantitative research methods were employed. Through a controlled online survey, approximately 200 materials managers rated each desired outcome statement for (i) its level of importance, and (ii) the degree to which it was satisfied, given the service offerings they were currently using. This data was used to run a variety of data analyses (Outcome-Based Segmentation, competitive analysis, etc.). The analyses resulted in the discovery of a large segment of materials managers that had approximately 50 underserved outcomes (see the opportunity landscape).

The analysis of this segment revealed a flaw in AMO's service delivery approach and in the process of obtaining ophthalmic lenses more generally. The process of communicating problems to AMO and its competitors frustrated materials managers. They were often unsure whom to contact to get a particular problem resolved because the issues they confronted ranged from delivery and lens consignment to invoicing and returns. AMO management recognized that delays often resulted because materials managers had to contact several people within AMO before finding someone who could help them. Matters were further complicated by the fact that the resolution of a given problem might require the involvement of several people and/or several layers of approval within AMO.

With knowledge of the customer's underserved outcomes, an ODI practitioner led a team of AMO sales, technical support, customer service, accounts payable, logistics, and IT infrastructure managers through the process of developing solutions to satisfy the most promising opportunities. Valuable solutions were conceptualized and later validated and implemented.

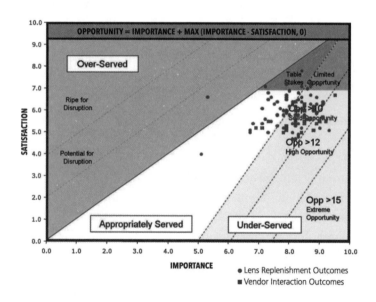

● Lens Replenishment Outcomes
■ Vendor Interaction Outcomes

The innovation and the impact

To improve its service delivery approach, AMO transitioned from a transaction approach to a relationship approach to customer service. As Rago explained, "Before, we had a first-in, first-out approach to customer service. A customer had no relationship with the person who happened to answer the phone when they called. Now, the top clients are automatically directed to a dedicated advocate who can handle anything that the customer needs. The next tier of clients go to regional customer care teams, or pods—a small team that works together to know the customer, and manage any concerns that the customer has."

AMO introduced advocates and regional customer care teams. Customers then had a single point of contact within AMO and a voice inside the company to address the range of issues they confront. If a customer issue required additional research, an AMO advocate or member of the care team had responsibility for problem resolution, ensuring that customers with tricky problems no longer had to navigate opaque internal processes without a guide. Physical proximity among team members of different functional areas also improved communication and coordination to resolve customer problems. As a result, the customer's problems were resolved faster and more thoroughly.

In addition, the customer service team assumed a more strategic role within AMO. Advocates and care team members reached out to customers on a regular basis to identify potential issues. Regional sales calls included customer care team members to ensure that everyone knew what changes were taking place and which accounts were being threatened. This enabled AMO to proactively head off potential account problems and better anticipate how to grow account revenues.

AMO's management team also learned that not having the right lenses on hand for a surgical case was a big problem for materials managers. Because this particular problem has more to do with the ongoing back-office operations of a surgical center than with vendor service and support, it had not occurred to AMO or its competitors to address it. But once the ODI methodology brought the problem to AMO's attention, the company was able to develop an advanced schedule-planning and inventory management software module that facilitated accurate and timely replenishment of lenses based on upcoming case needs, current inventory, and other considerations.

The implementation of these service offerings had immediate positive results:

- AMO's Net Promoter score increased by nearly 10 percent in the year following introduction of the service innovations.
- A MarketScope industry survey showed that industry perceptions of AMO's overall business practices and of the quality of its products and services has improved significantly since introduction of the innovations.

- AMO's corporate survey showed that its customer loyalty index improved by 14 percentage points in the year following introduction of the innovations.

Two years later, AMO was awarded the prestigious Omega Management NorthFace Award, which recognizes world-class customer satisfaction.

HUSSMANN

Discovering hidden growth opportunities

Hussmann decided to reexamine its LED product line. Used to illuminate refrigeration cases for cold beverages and perishable and frozen foods, the product line offered reduced operating costs—especially when compared with fluorescent lighting. But in the four years following the launch of the product line, Hussmann had seen little reaction from customers. Convenience stores, supermarkets, and warehouse stores simply didn't warm up to the idea.

"LEDs showed minimal volume and little impact on the lighting business," remarks Clay Rohrer, an innovation and business development manager at Hussmann. "We tried to penetrate the business for four years, and we were missing the boat."

Anshuman Bhargava, a Hussmann LED product manager and also an innovation and business development manager, notes, "We were going out and searching the globe for new technologies that seemed to make sense. They were always focused on energy or controls, which were trends in the market. We weren't tied to needs of the customer. We were tied to technologies."

LEDs, which offer energy efficiency, represented a potentially billion-dollar market, but customers were skeptical about the up-front costs and overall value of the technology. Hussmann knew that success would depend on the company's ability to uncover and inexpensively address specific customer needs so that Hussmann's LED product would stand out on performance dimensions that mattered to customers.

To find and exploit opportunities for competitive differentiation, Hussmann applied Strategyn's ODI methodology. Drawing on the responses of shoppers, store merchandisers, and executive merchandisers, Hussmann dissected the complementary jobs of those key groups.

"We had been selling refrigerated boxes, not merchandising solutions," Rohrer remarks. "Historically, we had left the merchandisers alone and focused more on the product procurement people. Now, we went to different levels of merchandisers and to the shoppers, and we combined insights from all these audiences."

This extensive, multi-audience effort resulted in the capture of over 300 desired outcome statements. Next, using ODI-based quantitative research techniques, Hussmann had 1,500 shoppers, 200 store merchandisers, and 50 executive merchandisers prioritize those outcomes.

Among the outcomes prioritized by executive merchandisers, many were underserved, as highlighted in the opportunity landscape. Of these unmet outcomes, eight related to display case lighting: for example, executive merchandisers wanted to increase the likelihood that the lighting would display the true product color and the likelihood that the lighting would be uniform.

These needs became the foundation for Hussmann's LED innovation and differentiation efforts.

The innovation and the impact

Knowing where to focus its efforts was the key to Hussmann's success. The team went through the eight underserved outcomes, developed engineering specifications for each and a new portfolio of LED lights, and then began systematically devising low-cost features that would dramatically improve customer satisfaction on each outcome.

Rohrer reports, "We used ODI to tweak an existing design and didn't have to redesign the whole thing. We looked at it from the ODI perspective of the job of illuminating products. What are the problem areas? What are the focus areas? Then we grouped the opportunities into common themes that we had to address to win the market. Uniform illumination, level of brightness, and energy efficiency were key things. We focused on them and developed solutions."

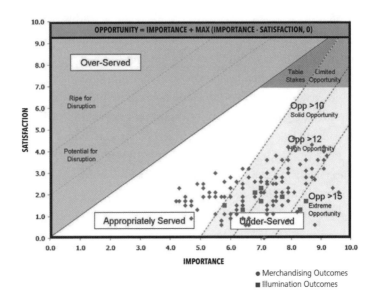

● Merchandising Outcomes
■ Illumination Outcomes

Hussmann created an innovative line of LED products— the EcoShine LED Lighting System—and focused its value proposition on satisfying the eight underserved outcomes in the merchandising of perishable food products. The EcoShine system matched competitors on certain outcomes for LEDs, such as energy efficiency and long life, but it was a breakthrough innovation because it added value on several new merchandising outcomes that competitors had overlooked. Hussmann advertises feature comparisons between the EcoShine line and its competitors on these specific outcomes. EcoShine boasts superior uniform horizontal and vertical lighting within a display case, reduced glare, and truer product colors (because the lighting is optimized for the display of meat, dairy, and produce). The product has been a hit in the market. **"In only one year, we've gone from a fraction of a digit to double digits in market share in North America,"** Bhargava notes. Backed by a strong sales commercialization effort, the product received favorable press coverage in industry publications such as Supermarket News, generated favorable buzz as a "home run" at trade shows, and created excitement among utility companies, who are providing incentives for customers to adopt this energy- efficient system.

In addition to generating immediate revenue growth (previously measured in thousands of dollars and now measured in tens of millions, according to Rohrer and Bhargava), the ODI process resulted in three other important benefits for Hussmann.

1. Cost reductions. Hussmann differentiated its LED products without increasing product cost—a prime objective. Rohrer describes how this was possible: "We made incremental changes to an existing platform in all the right areas, based on how customers measure value. We hit all the key outcomes at the right level without raising costs. In fact, we reduced costs dramatically because we were so focused on just changing the things that mattered."

2. Enhanced speed to market. Bhargava notes that having a prioritized list of customer needs, stated in clear, unambiguous language, made it possible to "move through the early stages [of product development] much more quickly … so that we could really get to work. We were able to translate the desired outcomes very clearly for engineering so that they understood what to develop. We didn't leave anything for them to guess at." He also notes that the insights gained through the process enabled Hussmann to set optimal prices based on the value of each SKU.

3. Enhanced credibility. The prioritized customer outcomes have changed the strategic dialogue within the firm. Rohrer states, "It is a whole different conversation with the executive team. It used to be a long decision process based on arguments over whether customers would buy some new product or not. 'Oh, did you think of this? Of that?' Now they see the exact need set and can evaluate how a solution might address those needs." Bhargava concurred, "ODI brings a lot of credibility. You no longer get questioned by internal stakeholders—operations and engineering, supply chain, sales, and so on."

Beyond these project benefits, ODI has created a fundamental shift in Hussman's innovation culture. As Rohrer describes it, "We've shifted the culture from a technology-driven company to a customer-needs-driven company."

PRACTICE

6.

BECOMING AN ODI PRACTITIONER

Jobs Theory intuitively makes sense, and Strategyn, through its application of ODI, has proven Jobs Theory is very effective in practice. With the contributions of leading academics like Clayton Christensen, and Jobs Theory champions and practitioners around the world, a new paradigm is on the horizon. I think it is safe to predict that companies will become more customer-centric, job-focused and outcome-driven. So what is next?

Many companies we've worked with over the years have wanted to put Jobs Theory and ODI into practice on a large scale. Most of them didn't want to be dependent on a third-party consulting firm over the long term for their ongoing success. Instead, they wanted to have and use their own practitioners and make Jobs Theory and ODI part of their DNA and organizational fabric. What our clients and other companies often want to know is this: "How do we put Jobs Theory and ODI into practice within our organization?"

In this chapter and the next, I will answer that question. While the next chapter addresses the needs of the organization, this chapter is written for the practitioner—the individuals that will take it upon themselves to apply Jobs Theory, practice ODI, and drive change in their organization.

In my days at IBM, I took on this role—the change agent, or the maverick as I was called. I was the internal consultant who wanted to help IBM find a better way to innovate. I took on the role of the practitioner as I tried to change the way people think about innovation. I remember how I appreciated the help I received from internal IBM supporters, my mentors and managers. I also remember how I'd wished that someone would come along and offer me the process, tools and instructions I would need to be successful. Now that I have the process, tools and instructions, I want to share them with you.

To that end, in the first quarter of 2017, Strategyn will make available to our clients a Jobs-to-be-Done Toolkit that will include the tools, templates, and instructions that Strategyn's internal ODI Practitioners use to effectively lead strategy and innovation engagements.

So, do you have what it takes to become an ODI Practitioner? Is becoming an ODI practitioner right for you? Let me help you decide.

Becoming an ODI Practitioner is not easy and it's not for everyone. Speaking as an ODI practitioner, however, I can tell you that, to me, it is the most fulfilling and rewarding career I could imagine. As an ODI Practitioner, you have the opportunity to:

- Work with the smartest and most inspiring people in business.
- Work on projects that span dozens of markets, learning more about each market than would otherwise be possible.
- Contribute to the creation of products and services that improve people's lives.
- Learn a valuable skill set that can be employed throughout your lifetime.
- Train your mind to think in a uniquely disciplined fashion.
- Contribute to the success of others and society as a whole.
- Have fun along the journey.

What does the ODI Practitioner do?

The ODI Practitioner is responsible for mastering the application of Jobs Theory and performing all aspects of the ODI process in a wide variety of contexts to meet the specific needs and expectations of the organization. An ODI Practitioner must be able to:

I. Initiate an ODI project.
II. Uncover the customer's needs.
III. Gather quantitative data.
IV. Discover hidden opportunities for growth.
V. Formulate the market strategy.
VI. Formulate the product strategy.

As I detail the ODI Practitioner's responsibilities for each of these 6 phases, I am going to reveal the **84-step process** that our Strategyn ODI Practitioners follow when they engage with clients. This insight will help you get a good sense of what it takes to execute an ODI project and the skill sets that are required to do so. Then you can decide if a career as a Jobs Theory and ODI practitioner in your organization is right for you.

I. INITIATE AN ODI PROJECT

In most companies that have adopted Jobs Theory and ODI, there is no shortage of possible applications. There is a good chance that you will be quickly overwhelmed with project opportunities.

In the first phase of an ODI engagement, the ODI practitioner must secure, scope, plan, and initiate the project. The goal in this phase of the engagement is to gain the project team's agreement on (i) the project plan and scope, (ii) who the customer is, (iii) the definition of the Job-to-be-Done, and (iv) the preliminary job map.

The 15 steps that the ODI Practitioner must take to effectively execute the first phase of a project are as follows:

1. Familiarize the organization with the benefits of JTBD theory and ODI.
2. Select a project to pursue using ODI.

3. Define the goals of the ODI project.
4. Scope the ODI project.
5. Define the project timeline.
6. Select the ODI project team.
7. Determine what types of needs must be captured for the project.
8. Create screener(s) to recruit candidates for job map interviews.
9. Recruit candidates for job map interviews.
10. Prepare the job map interview guide.
11. Understand the characteristics/structure of a job statement.
12. Conduct customer interviews to define the core functional Job-to-be-Done.
13. In complex markets, conduct quantitative research to define/validate the jobs that a platform solution gets done.
14. Conduct customer interviews to create the initial job map.
15. Gain the project team's preliminary agreement on the Job-to-be-Done, job map and project plan.

In this phase of the project the ODI practitioner is a project planner, a facilitator, a market researcher and a team builder.

II. UNCOVER THE CUSTOMER'S NEEDS

In the second phase of an ODI engagement, the ODI practitioner must capture a complete set of customer needs.

This includes all the desired outcomes on the core functional job along with the customer's related jobs and emotional jobs. In addition, the desired outcomes on any consumption chain jobs of interest and the buyer's financial metrics must be uncovered.

The goal in this phase of the engagement is to create the qualitative market research deliverable. It should contain a complete set of needs built around the Jobs-to-be-Done Needs Framework. The 18 steps that the ODI Practitioner must take to effectively execute the second phase of a project are as follows:

16. Create screener(s) to recruit candidates for outcome-gathering interviews.
17. Determine the format for conducting outcome-gathering interviews.
18. Prepare the outcome-gathering interview guide.
19. Recruit customer interview candidates for outcome-gathering interviews.
20. Understand the characteristics of a desired outcome statement.
21. Understand the structure of a desired outcome statement.
22. Conduct outcome-gathering interviews.
23. Uncover desired outcome statements on the Job-to-be-Done.
24. Net desired outcome statements (organize, refine, finalize).

25. Uncover related jobs.
26. Uncover emotional and social jobs.
27. Uncover relevant consumption chain jobs.
28. Uncover desired outcomes on relevant consumption chain jobs.
29. Uncover the buyer's financial desired outcomes.
30. Uncover factors that explain why some customers struggle more than others.
31. Gain the project team's agreement on the final job map, outcomes, and other statements.
32. Evaluate existing and pipeline products against needs (team exercise).
33. Create the qualitative research deliverable.

In this phase of the project the ODI practitioner is a project manager, a qualitative market research practitioner, and a team builder.

III. GATHER QUANTITATIVE DATA

In the third phase of an ODI engagement, the ODI practitioner must create, test, deploy and manage a survey that is fielded to a statistically valid sample of the customer population.

The goal in this phase of the engagement is to gather the data that is needed to (i) conduct outcome-based segmentation analysis, (ii) conduct competitive analysis, (iii) determine what customer needs and under-and overserved, (iv) determine the degree to which a need is under-and overserved, and (v) inform dozens of other downstream decisions that must be made to formulate the market and product strategy.

The 18 steps that the ODI Practitioner must take to effectively execute the third phase of a project are as follows:

34. Determine the unit of analysis for the quantitative survey.
35. Design the sample plan.
36. Determine how to weight the data.
37. Define any unique data analyses that are required.
38. Construct the screening questions for the quantitative survey.
39. Construct the profiling questions for the quantitative survey.
40. Construct the willingness-to-pay questions for the quantitative survey.
41. Format the outcome questions in the survey instrument for optimal results.
42. Gain the project team's agreement on the survey (instrument and questionnaire).
43. Select a vendor for data collection.
44. Translate the completed survey into required languages.
45. Program the survey for fielding.
46. Pilot/test the survey for fielding.
47. Field the survey.
48. Monitor the survey progress.

49. Prepare analytical tools for data analysis.
50. Receive the data from the data collection vendor.
51. Verify the data is valid (clean the data).

In this phase of the project the ODI practitioner is a project manager, a quantitative market research practitioner, and a third-party research manager.

IV. DISCOVER HIDDEN OPPORTUNITIES FOR GROWTH

In the fourth phase of an ODI engagement, the ODI practitioner must use the quantitative data that was collected in the previous phase to conduct **Outcome-Based Segmentation** analysis, competitive analysis and other analyses as required. The goal of this phase is to (i) run the analyses that are needed to address the key questions detailed in the scope of the project, and (ii) create the research deliverable.

The research deliverable explains what outcome-based segments were discovered, offers a description of each segment, reveals what hidden opportunities were discovered, and provides the information that is needed to formulate the market and product strategy.

The 10 steps that the ODI Practitioner must take to effectively execute the forth phase of a project are as follows:

52. Weight the quantitative data.
53. Create Outcome-Based Segmentation models.

54. Determine which segmentation model to use.
55. Conduct the analyses needed for segment profiling.
56. Determine what variables underlie the segmentation model (complexity factors).
57. Create a data-driven profile/description for each segment.
58. Determine what outcomes are underserved/overserved in each segment.
59. Determine the strengths and weaknesses of competitors in each segment.
60. Identify which outcomes are most influential in the customer's willingness-to-pay in each segment.
61. Complete commonly requested data analyses.
62. Create the opportunity discovery deliverable.

In this phase of the project the ODI practitioner is a project manager, a quantitative market research practitioner, a data analyst, and a strategist.

V. FORMULATE THE MARKET STRATEGY

In the fifth phase of an ODI engagement, the ODI practitioner uses the information resulting from the previously conducted data analyses to formulate a market strategy. The market strategy is usually constructed in conjunction with the project team.

The goal of this phase is to formulate, document, present, refine, and gain cross-functional agreement on the market strategy.

The 12 steps that the ODI Practitioner must take to effectively execute the fifth phase of a project are as follows:

63. Determine the strengths of existing and pipeline products (team exercise)
64. Determine what outcome-based segments and outcomes to target
65. Define the value proposition for each outcome-based segment
66. Define the value proposition for the product category
67. Determine what existing and pipeline products to target at each segment
68. Determine how to message each product
69. Determine how to integrate the new value proposition into existing company promotional channels/materials, e.g., the website, etc.
70. Propose an outcome-based digital marketing strategy, e.g., AdWords campaign, SEO optimization, etc.
71. Create a customer acquisition tool that assigns customers to segments
72. Gain the project team's agreement on the market strategy
73. Create the market strategy deliverable
74. Educate the sales/marketing team on executing the market strategy

In this phase of the project the ODI practitioner is a project manager, a data analyst, a strategist, a facilitator, and a team builder.

VI. FORMULATE THE PRODUCT STRATEGY

In the sixth and final phase of an ODI engagement, the ODI practitioner uses the information resulting from the previously conducted data analyses to formulate a product strategy. The product strategy, like the market strategy, is usually constructed in conjunction with the project team.

The goal of this final phase is to formulate, document, present, refine, and gain cross-functional agreement on the product strategy.

The 10 steps that the ODI Practitioner must take to effectively execute the fifth phase of a project are as follows:

75. Determine the weaknesses of existing and pipeline products (team exercise)
76. Determine what outcomes to target to address competitive weaknesses
77. Determine what value creation opportunities to address in each segment
78. Determine what cost reduction opportunities to address in each segment
79. Facilitate ideation to improve existing products
80. Facilitate ideation to improve pipeline products

81. Facilitate ideation to conceptualize new products/platforms
82. Gain the project team's agreement on the product strategy
83. Create the product strategy deliverable for each product
84. Create the product strategy deliverable for the product portfolio

In this phase of the project the ODI practitioner is a project manager, a data analyst, a strategist, a facilitator, and a team builder.

What skills are required to be a good ODI Practitioner?

Given the demanding responsibilities of the ODI Practitioner, we recommend that candidates meet all (or at least most) of the following qualifications:

- Process orientation and systems mentality.
- Skilled and experienced in qualitative and quantitative research practices.
- Superior creative problem-solving, analytical, and quantitative skills.
- Previous experience on a product team.
- Trained in Six-Sigma practices.
- Team leadership and group facilitation capabilities.

- Strong communication skills with ability to synthesize, document, and present knowledge effectively.
- Detail orientation. Highly organized.
- Strong knowledge of PowerPoint, Excel, and Word.

Now you know what it is like and what it takes to become an ODI Practitioner.

7.

TRANSFORMING THE ORGANIZATION

When companies think about building an innovation competency, they often think about training hundreds or even thousands of employees as part of a change management effort—they want their employees to think differently about innovation. When companies take this approach, they usually have the concept of innovation inextricably linked with broad cultural change in the organization.

What we have learned is that innovation (at least product and service innovation that results in revenue growth) should not be everyone's responsibility. It should be the responsibility of a small group of people—those who work to inform those that decide what markets to enter and grow and what products to place in the product development pipeline. The rest of the organization simply has to do what it has always done—that is, validate, prototype, design, build, create, ship, and launch new products. In my mind, training the entire organization for this purpose is not only time-consuming and costly, but it is an unnecessary activity. Most companies are great at creating products—they just aren't that great at creating the *right* products.

Many companies have reached the same conclusion, and this leads us to our recommended approach to building an innovation competency, which is to create a team of internal

ODI practitioners who will form the core of an Innovation Center of Excellence. This team, armed with the right tools and the appropriate training and support, are responsible for applying Jobs Theory and ODI practices to carefully selected markets and transforming the company into an outcome-driven organization.

The success of this team, and the innovation program, is dependent on using a customer-centric, data-driven innovation process that mitigates the risk of failure and leads to winning market and product strategies. If companies had to develop such a process on their own, it could take years, but fortunately Strategyn has already done that work. Outcome-Driven Innovation is that process. Once your organization is ready to test or adopt Jobs Theory and ODI, you are ready for the next step.

As in any endeavor, picking the right team is essential for success. Practices that we have seen work the best include building the team around or into an established Six Sigma program. We find that Six Sigma certified practitioners with qualitative and quantitative market research experience are often the best at understanding and applying ODI effectively within the organization. When armed with the right tools, they quickly begin transforming the organization.

PROGRAM OVERVIEW

Building an outcome-driven organization is best accomplished in three phases:

PHASE I	PHASE II	PHASE III
Understand Your Customer's Job to be Done	Discover Hidden Opportunities in Your Market	Use New Customer Insights to Drive Growth

Think about putting one product team through this process at a time, or putting many teams through simultaneously.

In Phase I, the cross-functional team for a selected product area participates in an intensive one-day workshop in which an ODI practitioner engages the team in a unique customer journey. For the first time the team sees its market through a "Jobs-to-be-Done" lens, and it learns what customer insights they need to drive outcome-driven decision-making. The team walks away with highly valuable customer insights derived from ODI-based qualitative research. The time commitment associated with this phase is relatively low, yet it moves the team well toward its goal of being outcome-driven.

In Phase II, the ODI practitioner leads the ODI-based quantitative research effort. With a statistically valid data set in hand, the ODI practitioner conducts outcome-based segmentation analysis, competitive analysis and others analyses needed to inform a market and product strategy. With the insights that result from these analyses, the company is able to make data-driven business decisions for years to come.

In Phase III, the ODI practitioner teaches managers and employees across the organization how to use these insights to formulate market and product strategies and to drive outcome-driven decision-making. Let's look at each phase in more detail:

PHASE I: UNDERSTAND YOUR CUSTOMER'S JOB-TO-BE-DONE

The best way to learn how to be customer-centric is to apply the basic Jobs-to-be-Done principles to your market. In Phase I, the cross-functional product team experiences the power of outcome-driven thinking in a one-day workshop in which they (i) learn the fundamentals of Jobs Theory and the ODI process, (ii) participate in a facilitated qualitative research discussion designed to obtain critical customer information, and (iii) begin to use their newfound insights to make outcome-driven business decisions in their market. The completion of Phase I will boost the team's ability to succeed at innovation because they leave in agreement on (i) who the customer is, (ii) what functional and emotional jobs the customer is trying to get done, (iii) the job map, (iv) what a customer need is, and (v) what the customer's needs are—the metrics customers uses to measure success and value when trying to get the job done.

The workshop employs the techniques and principles showcased in the *Harvard Business Review* article I co-authored titled "The Customer-Centered Innovation Map" (May 2008). Workshop participants typically include the product team (e.g., marketing, sales, planning, engineering, R&D), a handful of external customers, and the ODI practitioner, who leads the effort. The workshop is designed to shift the product team's thinking along a number of fronts (see the table below).

Expected Impact of Phase I: Qualitative Insights

Team Thinking Before Phase I	Team Thinking After Phase I
The product team disagrees on who the customer is (the buyer, user, installer, influencer).	The product team agrees on who the customers are and why.
The team defines the market from a product-centric perspective (around the product or technology).	The team defines the market from a customer-centric perspective (around the Job-to-be-Done).
The team doesn't know what job the customer is trying to get done.	The team agrees on what job the customer is trying to get done and on the job map.
The team can't agree on what a customer need is (purpose, structure, format, content).	There is cross-functional agreement on what a need is.
The team believes customers have latent needs and needs they can't articulate.	The team recognizes that customers can articulate their needs when they are defined around the Job-to-be-Done.
While the organization may collectively know most of the customer's needs, there is no agreed-upon list.	There is a single, agreed-upon list of customer needs that is shared across functions.

Upon completion of Phase I, the product team will share a common language of innovation and possess a unique set of customer insights (a job map and a set of desired-outcome statements) that it can use to make customer-centric marketing and development decisions. Because the job and customer outcomes are stable over time, these qualitative insights are an indispensible, long-term guide to success at innovation.

PHASE II: DISCOVER HIDDEN OPPORTUNITIES IN YOUR MARKET

In Phase II, the ODI practitioner creates a questionnaire (an online survey) that is used to collect the quantitative data. The survey is administered to a set of external customers (usually between 180 and 3000 people) that are representative of the population. The ODI practitioner uses a stringent set of quality standards that Strategyn has developed over the years to ensure only valid customer data is collected.

Once the data is collected, the ODI practitioner validates the responses and then conducts Outcome-Based Segmentation, competitive, market sizing, positioning, and other analyses.

With the data analyses completed, the ODI practitioner works with the team to apply this data to (i) better position existing products and services, (ii) improve existing products and services, and (iii) create new products and services that will deliver significant new value.

The research that occurs during Phase II is also designed to shift the product team's thinking along a number of fronts (see table below).

Expected Impact of Phase II: Quantitative Insights

Team Thinking Before Phase II	Team Thinking After Phase II
Nobody knows with certainty what customer needs are unmet and to what degree.	Everybody on the product team knows what needs are unmet and to what degree.
The segmentation model that managers use obscures differences in unmet customer needs (they focus on phantom targets).	Marketing and development managers use a segmentation model based on differences in unmet customer needs.
The company's competitive strengths and weaknesses relate to speeds and feeds.	The company's competitive strengths and weaknesses relate to addressing unmet needs.
The market strategy is based on personas and qualitative insights.	The market strategy is based on quantitative ODI-based market research. It is data-driven.
The product team does not agree on what market strategy to pursue.	The product team agrees on what market strategy to pursue and how to create customer value.
There is no agreement on what product and service concepts to pursue and invest in.	There is cross-functional agreement on what product concepts to pursue and invest in.

For years to come, the model built from this data set will help the team conceptualize and evaluate ideas for possible pursuit.

PHASE III: USE YOUR NEW CUSTOMER INSIGHTS TO DRIVE GROWTH

Having valuable customer data is one thing. Knowing how to use it is another. The types of data we capture and provide using our ODI-based research methods – job maps, opportunity landscapes, desired-outcome statements, outcome-based segments, opportunity scores, and so on – can be used to address dozens of challenges. For example, they can be used to:

- Create an outcome-driven digital marketing strategy, e.g., Google AdWords and SEO campaign, etc.
- Help the sales team deliver the right message to the right customer
- Inform your marketing communications program
- Reposition existing products around your competitive strengths
- Make improvements to existing products and services
- Conceptualize breakthrough, radical, and disruptive product ideas
- Drive decisions on research and development
- Inform merger and acquisition decisions

While many applications of the data are possible, using the data takes training. Phase III is dedicated to teaching managers and employees across the organization how to leverage their newfound customer insights. In both classroom training and hands-on workshops, the ODI practitioner teaches your product teams to make outcome-driven business decisions across a wide range of subjects. The education and training provided by the ODI practitioner are also designed to shift the product team's thinking along a number of fronts (see table below).

Expected Impact of Phase III: Implementation

Team Thinking Before Phase III	Team Thinking After Phase III
The team's focus is on beating the competition.	The team's focus is on helping customers get a job done better and/or more cheaply.
Innovation is about coming up with ideas and seeing if they address unmet customer needs.	Innovation is about uncovering unmet customer needs and finding solutions that address them.
Products are positioned around customer emotions.	Products are positioned around both functional jobs and outcomes and emotional needs.
The person with the loudest voice or the one in the most senior position influences the product team.	Customer data and facts influence the product team.
Technology, ideas, and capabilities drive strategy and decision-making.	Unmet customer needs dictate what ideas, technologies, and capabilities to invest in.
Decisions are made using qualitative customer insights and intuition.	Decisions are made using quantitative customer insights. Intuition is not acceptable.

Upon completion of Phase III, the product team will possess the ability to use ODI-based market research data and market and product strategy insights to consistently make business decisions that create customer value. They will have an outcome-driven mind-set, and your company will have successfully created a customer-centric culture of innovation. A product team can expect to complete its three-phase outcome-driven journey in four to six months.

Nothing is left to chance. *Or luck.*

Applying the **Outcome-Driven Innovation** process changes everything. It enables a company to:

- Discover hidden opportunities.
- Formulate market and product strategies that will undermine established leaders.
- Mitigate the risk of failure.
- Create what customers want.
- Predict what new products will win in the marketplace.
- Discover new markets.

With its 86 percent success rate, that is the power of the ODI process.

8.

THE LANGUAGE OF JOBS-TO-BE-DONE

A common language of innovation has the power to unite an organization in its effort to build a competency in innovation. The introduction of Jobs Theory presents companies with an opportunity to redefine the language of innovation from the customer's perspective; and an opportunity to understand and discuss innovation by seeing it through a new lens. These are the terms we use to define the concepts that comprise Jobs Theory and Outcome-Driven Innovation.

Brainstorming – An unbounded method of idea generation that encourages the creation of hundreds of ideas.

Business model canvas – A strategic management and entrepreneurial tool created by Alexander Osterwalder and Strategyzer that helps companies describe, design, challenge, invent, and pivot their business model.

Consumption chain jobs – The jobs that the product lifecycle support team must get done throughout the product lifecycle. These jobs include installation, set up, and storing, transporting, maintaining, repairing, cleaning, upgrading, and disposing of the product.

Creativity – The mental process by which an idea is triggered and conceived.

Customer – A constituent for whom the company chooses to create value. Key customers include the end user (the functional job executor), the purchase decision maker (buyer), and the product lifecycle support team (people who install, maintain, and repair the offering).

Customer need – A metric that customers use to measure the successful execution of a functional job or a consumption chain job. Synonymous with desired outcome.

Desired outcome – A metric that customers use to measure the successful execution of a functional job or a consumption chain job. Synonymous with customer need.

Differentiated strategy – A company pursues a differentiated strategy when it discovers and targets a population of underserved consumers with a new product or service offering that gets a job (or multiple jobs) done significantly better, but at a significantly higher price.

Discreet strategy – A company pursues a discrete strategy when it targets a population of "restricted" customers with a product that gets the job done worse, yet costs more.

Disruptive strategy – A company pursues a disruptive strategy when it discovers and targets a population of overserved customers or nonconsumers with a new product or service offering that enables them to get a job done more cheaply, but not as well as competing solutions.

Dominant strategy – A company pursues a dominant strategy when it targets all consumers in a market with a new product or service offering that gets a job done significantly better and for significantly less money.

Emotional jobs – Statements that describe the way customers want to be perceived or feel when executing a core functional job.

End user – This is a person who ultimately uses the product or service to execute the functional job the product is intended to perform. Also the functional job executor.

Financial outcomes – The financial metrics that the purchase decision maker uses to decide what product or service to purchase.

Functional Job-to-be-Done – The primary task or fundamental goal an end user is trying to accomplish or problem they are trying to resolve in a given situation.

Idea – An output of the creative process that defines a way in which specific unmet customer needs can be satisfied.

Ideas-first approach to innovation – An inherently flawed approach to innovation that starts with the generation of ideas and is followed by evaluation and filtering methods that determine which ideas customers like best without ever explicitly understanding their needs.

Industry – The collective set of companies that offer solutions to help customers get a job done.

Innovation – The process of devising a product or service concept that addresses the customer's unmet needs, thus enabling the customer to get a job done better and/or more cheaply.

Job executor – The group of people who are targeted for value creation. The job executor could be the functional job executor (end user), the purchase decision maker (buyer), or someone who executes a consumption chain job, such as the installer.

Job map – A visual depiction of a functional job, deconstructed into its discreet process steps. Unlike a process map, a job map does not show what the customer is doing (a solution view); rather, it describes what the customer is trying to get done (a needs view).

Job-to-be-Done – A task, goal or objective a person is trying to accomplish or a problem they are trying to resolve. A job can be functional, emotional or associated with product consumption (consumption chain jobs).

Jobs-to-be-Done Growth Strategy Matrix – A framework that illustrates when and how to deploy a differentiated, dominant, disruptive, discreet or sustaining growth strategy.

Jobs-to-be-Done Needs Framework – A visual depiction of the structure and relationship of all the customer inputs that are needed to effectively execute the innovation process.

Jobs-to-be-Done Theory – The notion that people buy products and services to get a job done and that new products and services win in the marketplace if they help customers get a job done better and/or more cheaply.

Market – A group of people (end users) and the core functional job or jobs they are trying to get done. Parents (a group of people) who are trying to pass on life lessons to their children (the Job-to-be-Done) constitute a market. Dental hygienists who clean patients' teeth and farmers who grow a crop also constitute markets.

Needs-first approach to innovation – An approach to innovation in which companies first uncover the customer's needs, then determine which are unmet, and then devise solutions to address those unmet needs.

New market – A new job that a group of customers want to get done because of changes in policy or conditions, scientific discoveries, or in support of a new technology, or a job that a significant group of customers now want to get done due to a demographic trend.

Market selection – The process of deciding what customers and Jobs-to-be-Done to target to create new revenue streams.

Market strategy – A plan that a company devises in order to achieve and maintain a unique and valued competitive position in a market. A market strategy includes the creation of a value proposition, product positioning and messaging, and the formulation of a digital marketing strategy.

ODI-based research methods – The qualitative and quantitative research methods that are integral to the Outcome-Driven Innovation process.

Opportunity – An unmet need; a desired outcome that is both important and poorly satisfied (underserved), or a desired outcome that is unimportant and very well satisfied (overserved).

Opportunity algorithm – The formula used to determine the degree to which a specific outcome or related or emotional job is under- or overserved. It is defined as opportunity = importance + max(importance – satisfaction, 0).

Opportunity landscape – A visual depiction of the opportunities that exist in a market and the degree to which the customer's desired outcomes are under-or overserved.

Outcome-based creativity triggers – A set of creativity triggers created by Strategyn that provide inventors with possible ways to address underserved unmet desired outcomes.

Outcome-Based Segmentation™ – A method by which segments of customers with uniquely different underserved desired outcome can be discovered, sized and targeted.

Outcome-driven brainstorming – The process of conceptualizing new platforms, business models, and features that address underserved segments and desired outcomes discovered through the use of ODI-based research methods.

Outcome-Driven Innovation® (ODI) – A strategy and innovation process that ties customer-defined metrics (desired outcomes) to the Job-to-be-Done, making value creation (and innovation) measurable and predictable. The process employs qualitative, quantitative, and market segmentation methods that reveal hidden opportunities for growth. ODI has an 86 percent success rate—a five-fold improvement over the industry average.

Overserved market segment – A segment of customers with a majority of desired outcomes that are unimportant and well satisfied.

Process of disruptive innovation - The introduction of a series of products, the first of which employs a disruptive strategy that gets the job done worse and more cheaply, followed by a series of products that build on that technology platform, with more and more features, until the newest offerings get the job done better and more cheaply.

Product lifecycle support team – People (customers) who help install, set up, store, transport, maintain, repair, clean, upgrade, and dispose of the product, and perform other support services as necessary.

Purchase decision maker – The person responsible for executing the "buying" job: seeking out and evaluating alternative offerings and deciding which to buy.

Qualitative research – Market research methods used to uncover the customer's desired outcomes and other inputs that comprise the Jobs-to-be-Done needs framework.

Quantitative research – Market research methods used to gather the statistically valid data needed to conduct Outcome-Based Segmentation analysis and other data analyses that comprise the ODI process.

Related jobs – Functional jobs the end user is trying to get done in conjunction with the core functional job. Getting more jobs done on a single platform make the platform more valuable.

Strategyn – The company that pioneered Jobs Theory and created the Outcome-Driven Innovation process.

Strategyn Jobs-to-be-Done toolkit - A toolkit that includes a starter-workshop and the materials, templates and tools that Strategyn's consultants use to execute ODI-based projects for Strategyn clients.

Sustaining strategy - A company pursues a sustaining strategy when it introduces a new product or service offering that gets the job done only slightly better and/or slightly cheaper.

Underserved market – A market in which the majority of the customer's desired outcomes are important and poorly satisfied.

Unmet need – A desired outcome or related or emotional job that is both important and poorly satisfied.

9.
LEARN MORE

A BRIEF HISTORY OF JOBS-TO-BE-DONE

1962
Theodore Levitt said, "people don't want a quarter-inch drill, they want a quarter-inch hole."

1984
IBM's PCjr is introduced into the market and immediately called a flop. The failure inspired Tony Ulwick to try to create an innovation process that mitigates the risk of failure.

1990
Ulwick has an epiphany: if a company focused on the process of creating a "quarter inch hole" instead of creating a better drill, it could apply Six-Sigma principles to study the underlying process and offer a new path to innovation.

1991
The Total Quality Group is founded by Tony Ulwick. The goal of the company is to put his new theory and innovation process (CD-MAP) into practice.

1992
Ulwick uses his new process to help Cordis Corporation create a new line of angioplasty balloons. This is the first application of Ulwick's innovation process.

1994

As a result of Ulwick's work, Cordis Corporation released 19 new products, all of which became number one or two in the market. Cordis's market share increased from 1% to over 20%. Ulwick validated that his innovation process works.

1996

Ulwick filed the first of twelve patents to be granted on his innovation process. The patents describe a method by which new product concepts are constructed and evaluated around the metrics customers use to measure success when executing a task or a process.

1997

Ulwick applies his Outcome-Based Segmentation method to Motorola's radio market. Segmenting the market around unmet outcomes leads to the creation of the TalkAbout radio and a new professional radio that accelerated the division's growth from 0% to 18%.

1999

Ulwick changes his company name to Strategyn and the name of his process to Outcome-Driven Innovation (ODI).

1999

Ulwick introduces his ODI process to Harvard Business School professor Clayton Christensen in a series of meetings in Cambridge where he explains the benefits of focusing on the underlying process, not the product or customer.

2000

Ulwick completes his 50th engagement using the Outcome-Driven Innovation process.

2002

Harvard Business Review publishes "Turn Customer Input Into Innovation". Authored by Tony Ulwick, the article introduced the ODI process and used the Cordis example to illustrate its effectiveness.

2002

Harvard Business Review recognizes Strategyn's thinking as one of the best business ideas of the year, declaring it one of "the ideas that will profoundly affect business as we forge ahead in today's complex times."

2003

In his book *The Innovator's Solution*, Clayton Christensen introduced the notion that "people buy products and services to get a job done". This book popularized what has become known as "Jobs-to-be-Done" theory. Professor Christensen graciously cites Strategyn and Ulwick as originators of these practices and their work in job and outcome-based thinking, market segmentation, and the ODI process.

2004

Strategyn publishes 3 landmark case studies that demonstrate how ODI was used to successfully drive growth at Kroll Ontrack, Microsoft, and Bosch.

2005

Tony Ulwick introduces *What Customers Want*, a best-selling business book published by McGraw Hill that explains how Outcome-Driven Innovation transforms Jobs-to-be-Done theory into practice.

2005

Harvard Business Review publishes "Marketing Malpractice: The Cause and the Cure." Authored by Clayton Christensen, the article explained how a jobs focus can help a company in growing a product category.

2006

Ulwick completes his 150th engagement using the Outcome-Driven Innovation process.

2007

Strategyn releases additional case studies demonstrating the effectiveness of ODI.

2008

Harvard Business Review publishes "The Customer-Centered Innovation Map". Authored by Tony Ulwick and Lance Bettencourt, the article introduced the "job map"; a framework that helps to deconstruct and understand the Job-to-be-Done.

2008

MIT Sloan Management Review publishes "Giving Customers A Fair Hearing". Authored by Tony Ulwick, the article explained how Jobs-to-be-Done theory provides a framework around which to define, structure, gather and organize customer needs.

2010

An independent track record study reveals that the use of the Outcome-Driven Innovation process results in an 86% success rate, which is five times the industry average.

2010

Johnson & Johnson's Ethicon Endo Surgery uses ODI to inform the creation of the harmonic blade. The product wins the prestigious Edison Gold Award for innovation.

2013

Ulwick completes his 250th engagement using the Outcome-Driven Innovation process.

2015

Ulwick is granted his twelve patent on the innovation process.

2016

Clayton Christensen writes "Competing Against Luck", a book that details how Jobs-to-be-Done theory transforms innovation from a game of chance to a more predictable process.

2016

Tony Ulwick writes "Jobs-to-be-Done, Theory to Practice", a book that explains how companies can dramatically improve their innovation success rates by adopting jobs-to-be-done theory and ODI.

2016

Strategyn celebrates 25 years as a leading strategy and innovation consulting firm.

ONLINE LEARNING RESOURCES

Strategyn.com
AnthonyUlwick.com
JTBDinstitute.org

VIDEOS AND WEBINARS

youtube.com/strategyn

BOOKS AND ARTICLES

What Customers Want: Using Outcome-Driven Innovation to Create Breakthrough Products and Services
by **Anthony Ulwick**
McGraw-Hill (2005)

Turn Customer Input Into Innovation
by **Anthony Ulwick**
Harvard Business Review – January 2002

Prescription for Health Care Cost Reform
by **Anthony Ulwick**, **Clayton Christensen**, **Jerome Grossman**
Harvard Business Review – March 2003

Do You Really Know What Your Customers Are Trying to Get Done?
by **Anthony Ulwick**
Harvard Business Review – March 2003

Lost in Translation
by **Anthony Ulwick**
Harvard Business Review – May 2004

Giving Customers A Fair Hearing
by **Anthony Ulwick** and **Lance Bettencourt**
MIT Sloan Management Review – April 2008

The Customer-Centered Innovation Map
by **Lance Bettencourt** and **Anthony Ulwick**
Harvard Business Review – May 2008

ABOUT

Tony Ulwick is the pioneer of Jobs-to-be-Done theory, the inventor of the Outcome-Driven Innovation (ODI) process, and the founder of the strategy and innovation consulting firm Strategyn. He is the author of *What Customers Want* (McGraw-Hill) and numerous articles in *Harvard Business Review* and *Sloan Management Review*.

CONTACT

tony@strategyn.com

www.strategyn.com
www.anthonyulwick.com

SPECIAL THANKS

A special thanks goes to Perrin Hamilton for his contributions in creating the Jobs-to-be-Done Growth Strategy Matrix and writing Chapter 3, and also to Christian Sarkar who has been amazing through each step of the publishing process. I'd also like to thank my entire team at Strategyn for their support and commitment to advancing the process of innovation. Lastly, I want to thank my wife Lindsay for making my life perfect.